Windsor Castle
in the History of the Nation

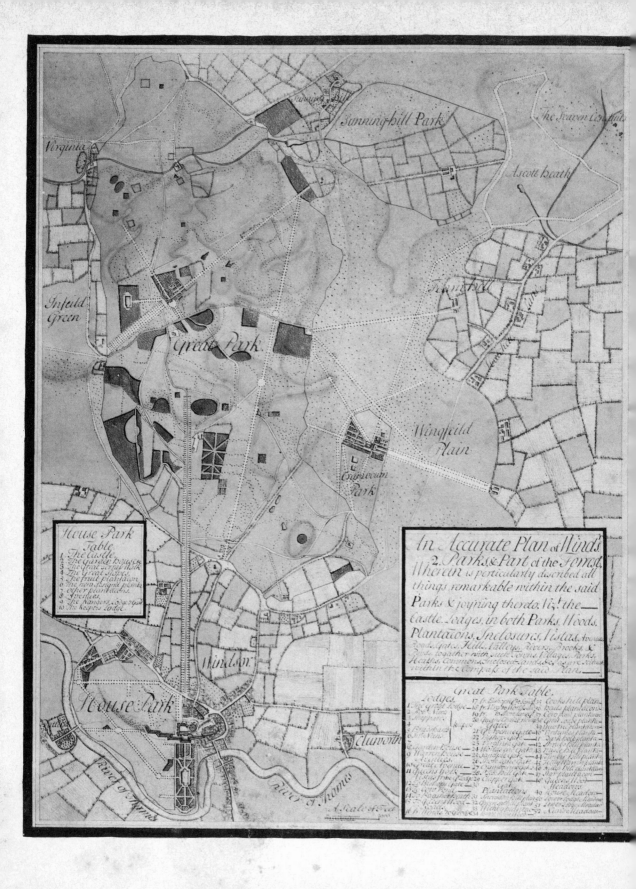

A.L. ROWSE

WINDSOR CASTLE
IN THE HISTORY OF THE NATION

WEIDENFELD AND NICOLSON
London

Designed by Margaret Downing for
George Weidenfeld and Nicolson Ltd

Filmset by Keyspools Ltd, Golborne, Lancs
Printed in Great Britain

ISBN 0 297 76712 7

To
Ambassador Walter Annenberg
in recognition of
his many benefactions to Britain

Acknowledgments

Photographs and illustrations were supplied or are reproduced by kind permission of the following. The pictures on pages 1, 82/3, *110/11*, 155, 158, 172, 174, 177, 182/3, 184, 188, *193*, *194/5*, *196*, 213, 224, 227, are reproduced by gracious permission of H.M. the Queen; on page 50 by courtesy of the Duke of Norfolk, Arundel Castle; on pages 30 and 31 by courtesy of the Dean and Chapter of Canterbury Cathedral (photo John Freeman); on pages 32/3 by kind permission of the Provost and Fellows of Eton College, Windsor; on pages 101, 121, by kind permission of the Warden and Fellows of All Souls College, Oxford; on page 151 by kind permission of Commander Campbell Johnston. Aerofilms Ltd: 10/11; J. Allen Cash: 98, 199; Bodleian Library: *17*; British Museum: 14, 21, *36* (photo John Freeman), 42, 49, 70, *112* (above), 128/9, 156/7, 166, 191, *229*, *230/1*; A. F. Kersting: 8, 15, 34, 37, 223, *232* (above); National Gallery, London: 148/9; National Portrait Gallery: 72, 124, 132, 135, 142, 163, 200, 219; Phoebus Picture Library: 36, 102/3, *109*; Radio Times Hulton Picture Library: 26/7, 96/7, 107, 118/19, 169, 210/11, 216/17, 236, 240, 242/3, 246, 248; Royal Academy of Art: 206; Victoria and Albert Museum: 77, *112* (below); William Gordon Davis: 181; from Windsor Castle by W. H. St. John Hope: 65; Woodmansterne Ltd (photo Nicholas Servian): *18*, *35*.

Numbers in italic indicate colour illustrations.

Picture research by Philippa Lewis and Annette Brown.

Contents

Henry VIII's Gateway at Windsor.

I
Medieval Power and Chivalry

WINDSOR Castle provides the image most people would associate with the idea of England – more than, say, the Tower of London or even Westminster Abbey. There it is high on its tufted ridge, the long medley of walls and towers and buildings, royal and ecclesiastical – epitome of monarchy, state and church – dominated by the great Round Tower, with outsize flag at mast, all mirrored in the Thames below, along which has flowed so much of English history.

In spite of the accretions of the last century, its profile is singularly unchanged since the later Middle Ages, though from whatever angle one approaches it a different aspect is revealed, opening up what vistas to the informed imagination. Most impressive, and slightly forbidding, it looks from the river, frowning cliff-like down upon the steep northern escarpment: a long wall of ramparts topping the horizon, its most secure and defensive side where in the upper bailey were the lodgings of the medieval kings. Going up Thames Street is more familiar: here the Castle is married to the town – still more so in former days when houses crept up to the very walls, in the manner of a castle in a French town.

Then there is the sprawling approach up to Henry VIII's gate, with the medley of history in its variegated buildings – Henry II and Henry III's walls and turrets, Edward IV's chapel of St George, George IV's Gothick façades and fantastic machicolations. Or the trimmed parterres and terraces, the sunken garden, looking up to the East Front, private residence of the sovereign. Grandest of all, the distant view from the south across Great Park and Long Walk, the Regency fantasy conceived by George IV and carried out by Wyatville, the roofscape unlike any other in the world, that carries the image of Windsor Castle to all parts of it.

Today we have new variations of the historic image to offer. As one sees it, leaving the country in a plane for America, the grey mass of stone-masonry set in greenery; walls, courts, quadrangles; paths, straight and diagonal; avenues, trees, park, woods; sunlight or shadow, white, grey, blue, on the Round Tower; then into the clouds. Or perhaps one strains for a glimpse from a rail-

9

Overleaf: 'The grey mass of stone masonry set in greenery: walls, courts, and quadrangles; paths, straight and diagonal; avenues, trees, park, woods; sunlight or shadow, white, grey, blue, on the Round Tower.'

way-carriage on the way to London, across the unending waste and squalor of new industry, watches for a brief break in the factories and mean tenements, and – if one is lucky – catches a fleeting sight of that noble outline looking greyly out over the dereliction and indignity of our time.

Paradoxically, this English pile, characteristically eclectic, we owed to the French, to whom we are largely indebted for our medieval civilisation. The Anglo-Saxon kings, ending with Edward the Confessor, had their residence and held their court at Old Windsor, in the water-meadows a couple of miles away. There William the Conqueror succeeded them; but his strategic eye saw that this bare chalk cliff was the only strong point for a fortress between London and Wallingford. He proceeded to raise a motte, with keep and wooden palisade, as he had done within the Roman bastion of the City-wall by the river in founding the Tower of London. Contrary to legend again, the Romans made nothing of the site – though a coin of the time of Agricola turned up in a Windsor garden not long ago, lost by what trader or shopkeeper, citizen or soldier, when or who?

The site itself was, and is, wonderful, dominating the river, with the forest behind, water-meadows and Eton in front, which the later Middle Ages also decorated with the gathered turrets and pinnacles of its Chapel. What a noble assembly altogether – and still dedicated to the uses and functions for which they were created! The kings have departed from the palace-monastery of the Escorial; the Emperors have gone from Hofburg and Schönbrunn, from Kremlin and Winter Palace; the Louvre and Versailles are museums, the Tuileries no more; Sans Souci and the Hradschin are under the Communist heel. But Windsor goes on fulfilling the functions for which it was created: residence of the sovereign, the panoply of monarchy, the visible embodiment of Church – with St George's Chapel – and service to the state, since it is the home of the Order of the Garter, and with some military colouring in the residences of the Poor Knights.

Like English history – except for the horror of the Civil War – all very continuous and unbroken.

We must remember that the Thames – with no locks below Maidenhead till about 1800 – was the principal route for traffic throughout the Middle Ages and later. As also a plentiful supplier of fish, eels and salmon, up to the same date. It was too the northern boundary of the Forest – the large area the kings and others enjoyed for their hunting, extending over east Berkshire, and into Surrey and northern Hampshire. This was not all wooded, as people nowadays take the word 'forest' to mean – 'forest' simply meant the wild country *outside* the enclosed and paled park. It was an expanse of heath country, including the sandy stretches of Sandhurst and Bagshot, with some woodland and many coverts for game. When Charles Kingsley first went as rector to Eversley in northern Hampshire there were old parishioners who remembered poaching the deer that strayed over from Windsor Forest.

William the Conqueror's son, Henry I, was the first to build a residence within the upper bailey, and to hold court there at Whitsun, 1110. Here too he married his second wife, Adeliza of Lorraine, and entertained David, King of Scots. Having no son, Henry summoned his nobles to Windsor in 1127 to swear allegiance to his daughter, the haughty Empress Maud. No success as a ruler herself – it took a man, and a pretty tough one, to rule the country in those days – her son succeeded as Henry II. He made the Castle much stronger as a fortress, surrounding it with stone walls (which we can still see on the west side from Thames Street); in 1172 he built the Round Tower and a wall from it across the narrow waist, dividing the upper ward from the lower.

We all remember the brood of fighting, quarrelling sons the Angevin Henry II had – the young Henry, Richard Coeur-de-Lion, Geoffrey, whose son Arthur his uncle John murdered. It is said that in his chamber in the royal lodgings at Windsor the king had a picture painted on the wall, of an old eagle being preyed upon by four young ones. If so, no wonder!

King John seems to have been fond of Windsor and spent as much time there as his feverish restlessness allowed him. He seems to have had a good time there, politics apart, with all the provision of pheasants, partridges, chickens, salmon, pork, bacon and beans made for him. In addition consignments of wine were sent up the Thames, though there was a vineyard on the southern slopes, for the climate was warmer then. Once John even sent an urgent request for a book, 'The Romance of the History of England': was this possibly Geoffrey of Monmouth's *History of the Kings of Britain* which spread the Arthurian story all over medieval Europe?

John was a good deal of a drunkard and killed his nephew Arthur of Brittany – an older brother's son – in the castle of Rouen. A favourite companion, William of Briouze, was there at the time and knew too much. When he lost favour John tried to exterminate the whole family. William escaped him, but he got hold of Briouze's wife and son – and starved them to death in Windsor Castle. The chronicler says that when the bodies were found, the mother had gnawed the cheeks of her son in the pangs of starvation. Such were the Middle Ages; but the twentieth century has provided similar examples of man's inhumanity – in Germany, of course.

King John got his comeuppance at Runnymede, some three miles downstream, with Magna Carta humiliatingly imposed upon him by his barons and the Church. Every day in the week from 15 to 23 June 1215, he rode over from

Left: Magna Carta, humiliatingly imposed on King John. 'Every day from 15–23 June 1215, he rode over from the castle to receive bitter drafts of the medicine he so richly deserved.'

Henry III's doorway – 'the exquisite scrolled iron-work of the door, once covered with scarlet gesso still signed by the maker 'Gilebertus', in spite of all the destruction of the centuries.'

the Castle to receive bitter draughts of the medicine he so richly deserved. When next year he failed to abide by his undertakings – and indeed no-one could trust such a man – the barons called in the French king to take over his throne. Windsor Castle stood a three-months' siege, without being reduced. In the end the siege was raised, when the besiegers went off in pursuit of John in flight towards Cambridge, losing the crown-jewels in the Wash, and to his ignominious end at Newark.

It remained for his son, Henry III, to pick up the pieces.

Henry III was hardly more successful than his father as a politician, but he was, what was much better, an aesthete with a loving sense of beauty. To him we owe

Westminster Abbey. In addition he did a great deal of building and decoration within the Tower of London. Windsor he made one of the most splendid castles of Europe, Matthew Paris tells us. We can still see much of his work in the western walls and round towers dominating Thames Street.

Since he made it a principal residence from 1236 he had the immensely deep well excavated within the Round Tower, and another well each for the upper and lower wards. The royal lodgings were always on the most defensible northern side of the upper ward. Henry added additional chambers for himself and his Queen, marble pillars, with paintings and stained glass richly dight. On the site of the present Albert Memorial Chapel he built a chapel, of which we can still see exquisite remains: six Purbeck columns, the arches of the narthex now forming the vestibule; the exquisite scrolled ironwork of the door, once covered with scarlet gesso, still signed by the maker 'Gilebertus', in spite of all the destruction of the centuries. To the decoration of this chapel of St Edward Henry gave a large silver-gilt image of the Virgin, and an armoured one of St George (who, we are now told on higher authority, never existed). Nevertheless *ars vincit omnia* – art makes up for everything.

A number of Henry's children were born here; the Queen was apt to remain with them at Windsor while the King prowled round the country on necessary business. From the simple entries in the Close Rolls we can deduce the life: sums from alien lands in the hands of Peter of Geneva to be paid over for the children's necessities. Of the daily catch of lampreys from the Severn in 1248 two-thirds to be sent to the King in Norfolk, one-third to the Queen at Windsor. Provision of pork, roebucks, salted stags, wine for the household; bream and small pike for stocking the stews. Four serjeants-of-arms were in attendance – all was on a smaller, domestic scale; payments are made for their wages, gowns and firewood. When a man was hanged for homicide, his sword was forfeit: the King gave it to a retainer.

But, since this was the Middle Ages, the grandest efforts were reserved for religion. For the new chapel there were to be four bells, painted pictures and *vexilla* (banners); a chalice and hanging basin, rich copes and vestments, illuminated service books. Outside, the cloister was to be paved, panelled and decorated. Nor were the leprous brethren and sisters overlooked.

To come to dreary, but necessary, politics – we are reminded that Windsor has been the scene of many historic decisions: far more so, for example, than the Tower of London. Henry III was hardly more successful a politician than his father, but of course a less brutal, more congenial, character. In the chops and changes of his long reign we find him holding Councils at Windsor, in 1236 and 1244, to advise him upon the ever-pressing demand for reforms in his government – he was, of course, extravagant, if to good purpose and was

Right: The Gough Map (c. 1360). The earliest road map showing Windsor and its environment.

surrounded by foreign favourites who probably exemplified more cultivated tastes than his militant barons. In October 1254, while Henry was away in France, his brother Richard of Cornwall – who had bought what he hoped would be the succession to the Holy Roman Empire out of his royalties on Cornish tin – held a 'parliament' at Windsor, with the barons of the Exchequer present; so one may surmise that the Crown's pressing need for cash was under discussion.

When conflict between Crown and baronage, under the leadership of the great Simon de Montfort, reached its climax, the Opposition summoned the knights of the shires in 1261 to meet at St Albans. The King countered by ordering them to meet at Windsor, where he proposed to treat with the insurgents from a position of strength. Two years later the Court was taken by surprise, with the King away in the Tower. Young Prince Edward at once made for Windsor to hold it as a centre of resistance; but the barons in control of the City made him disband his foreign mercenaries, and the Prince had to surrender Windsor under threat of attack. In the autumn French support enabled Edward to re-occupy Windsor, where the King joined him. Thence he summoned an equal number of barons from each side to work out a settlement.

Men being what they are, the battlefield was the only effective arbiter. Next year, 1264, Henry was totally defeated at Lewes, and for the next year de Montfort was virtually in control of the kingdom. Windsor was surrendered, and Edward's young bride, Eleanor of Castile, ordered to leave with her infant daughter. In August next year there was a complete reversal at the battle of Evesham, where Simon fell, his forces decimated. Henry and Edward regained control of their kingdom; 'and thus time's whirligig brings in his revenges'.

Ordinances to re-establish peace on the Crown's terms were issued from Windsor, and thither Henry summoned his feudal host to reduce London to submission. The citizens, considering discretion the better part of valour, sent their Mayor and forty leading spirits to Windsor under a safe-conduct. There they were kept in close confinement in the Round Tower – it must have been very close – for twenty-four hours, and afterwards were herded in the lower bailey for several days before release.

It is more revealing to follow the sequel in the fate of individuals. Edward had captured the castellan of Dunster and sent him to Windsor, where he was 'heavily fettered, so that the earl of Derby, there in captivity, might not be without a companion'. Simon's son, Guy de Montfort, wounded and taken prisoner at Evesham, was carried to Windsor, thence to Dover. From Dover he escaped – to perpetrate the murder of Richard of Cornwall's son, Henry, in the cathedral at Viterbo, in revenge for his father's death at Evesham. Simon's daughter, Eleanor, had been betrothed to Llewelyn, the last independent

Left: The Knights' Stalls showing the stall plates in St George's Chapel.

Welsh Prince. A girl of thirteen, she was sent into exile. Ten years later, in 1275, she set out to marry the Prince in Wales, but was captured in the Bristol Channel, and taken to confinement at Windsor. It was not until Llewelyn submitted to Edward, now king, that he would allow the marriage to go forward. It took place with much splendour, three years later, before the doors of Worcester cathedral, and the couple departed in happiness to Wales. In 1282 Eleanor died in childbirth; the same year Llewelyn was slain, and the independent principality of Wales extinguished. His head was brought to the Tower of London, his gold circlet offered to the shrine of Edward the Confessor in Westminster Abbey.

With the reign of Edward III (1327–77) we come to the first grand period still recognizable to any visitor to Windsor, both in its buildings, still more in its visual history. For he was the founder of the Order of the Garter, the home of which is St George's Chapel, where the annual commemoration is still observed on 23 April – the procession of the Sovereign and Knights of the Garter, service in Chapel, observed now by thousands and millions, in the age of tourism and television.

Known as Edward of Windsor in his youth, for he had been born there on 13 November 1312, the King was specially attached to the place of his birth and baptism. He is said to have spent altogether some £50,000, in the currency of his time, upon transforming the Castle 'into the fortified palace it has since remained'. He scoured the country for masons, carpenters, glaziers, building labour. Most of his fabric has since disappeared – a large remodelling of the royal lodgings, though we can see what the great hall looked like from Hollar's admirable engraving of a Garter Feast within it. There is still Edward's work in undercroft and corridors beneath Wyatville's piles, vaulted vestry, treasury and porch within the present Deanery; parts of the canons' cloister with its Decorated tracery, the gatehouse into the inner bailey with its stone-vaulted roofs.

All this provided the physical frame for Edward's chivalric projects.

We have seen that the Middle Ages had a cult of Arthurianism, and the Order of the Garter really sprang out of that. As we can see from Froissart's fabled and embellished account. 'About this time [the 1340's] the King of England resolved to rebuild and beautify the great castle of Windsor, which King Arthur had first founded in time past, and where he had erected and established that noble Round Table from whence so many gallant knights had issued forth, and displayed the valiant prowess of their deeds at arms over the world.' So the Middle Ages thought, or affected to believe – the Arthurian story went all over Christendom, in various languages and divers arts.

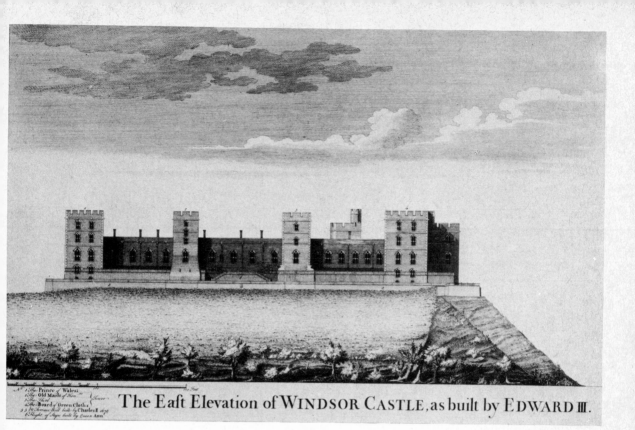

The East Elevation of WINDSOR CASTLE, as built by EDWARD III.

The West Elevation of the KEEP, or ROUND TOWER of WINDSOR CASTLE, Built by EDWARD III

References ¹ A Section of the North ... ² The Entrance to the upper Court ... ³ The Stair Case to the Keep ... ⁴ The Moat ... ⁵ The Curtain ... ⁶ The Keep ... ⁷ An Ancient Going Way from the Keep to ... ⁸ The Mask of Hon. or Front Stairs to Rampart Wall

St George's Hall, built
by Edward III; an
engraving by Hollar
for Ashmole's *Order of
the Garter*.

Edward seems to have begun with a project of a Round Table, after a grand supper he gave to his peers and knights in January 1344. There was to be a Round Table of some three hundred knights, and he began laying the foundations for a large circular space in the upper ward, evidently for jousting. The project was not proceeded with, for the French war intervened. Edward laid claim to the French crown, quartering the lilies of France on his shield, for he had a very near claim through his mother. He was himself French, like all the kings since the Conquest; and so were half his baronage. They all spoke French and belonged to a cosmopolitan military aristocracy – this must be remembered when we consider the depredations they made upon the fair fields of France and the spoils they brought back to the island kingdom their forebears had originally conquered.

At the end of August 1346 Edward won the shattering victory of Crécy, where his son, the Prince of Wales, in black armour, won his spurs leading the van. The youth was sixteen – to become famous all over Europe as a warrior, the Black Prince. The King of Bohemia was killed in the battle; the Prince took his badge, the ostrich feathers, and the motto in German, '*Ich Dien*' (i.e. I serve.) If you want to see what he looked like in later life, there he lies on his tomb in Canterbury cathedral, the leopards of England and the lilies of France across his armoured chest, the helm he wore suspended above his effigy. A year later, after a long siege, Calais surrendered: every English schoolboy used to know the famous episode of 'the burghers of Calais' (sculpted by Rodin) – not to be expected today.

On their return King and Prince celebrated their victories with a series of splendid tournaments through the autumn and winter of 1347–8. And now Edward's plans took more practical shape for a smaller Order of knighthood, containing essentially his and the Black Prince's young companions, based on Windsor. This was the purpose of the building programme in the lower ward. The new chapel was built, on the site of the present Albert Memorial Chapel; it was to be served by a college of twenty-four canons, with a warden, for whom lodgings and a cloister were provided. There were to be twenty-four poor knights, pensioned off from the wars; and twenty-four (later twenty-six) companions of the sovereign, who was always to be Sovereign of the Order they constituted. The essence of the Order was military; promotion to it was the recognition of service in arms, not in Council or Parliament – that demanded other abilities. (It is characteristic of today that promotion to it should be accorded to that great warrior – at least, for chastity – Lord Longford.)

There is no reason for doubting the ancient tradition as to how the Order came by its name – there is usually something in a very old and tenacious tradition. Edward III was as gallant as he was handsome, and a number of ladies shared his favours. At one of his entertainments one of them dropped a blue garter; Edward appropriated it, and put it on his own leg with '*Honi soit qui mal y pense.*' ('Shame to him who thinks ill of it.') It became the motto of the Order; how otherwise to account for it if something of the sort had not happened?

More interesting are the companions, the founder-members: they offer a roll-call of the chivalry of the time. With Edward and his son were their cousin Lancaster, who governed Aquitaine for the King and had been at the siege of Calais; the Beauchamp Earl of Warwick who led the van under the Prince at Crécy; the Montacute Earl of Salisbury, Sir Ralph Stafford, Sir Roger Mortimer, Sir Hugh Courtenay, Sir Thomas Holland had all served at Crécy or Calais, or both. Sir John Beauchamp had fought at the thundering naval victory of Sluys. Lord Lisle, Lord Mohun, Lord Grey of Rotherfield – whose mouldering walls we still see at Rotherfield Greys in Oxfordshire – were others. One of the most celebrated of them all was Sir John Chandos, descended from a companion of the Conqueror, and a life-long comrade-in-arms of the Black Prince, in whose service he was eventually killed in France, mourned by both sides. His epitaph long remained:

> Je, Jean Chandos, des Anglais capitaine,
> Fort chevalier, de Poitou sénéchal,
> Après avoir fait guerre très lointaine
> Au roi français tant à pied qu'à cheval,
> Et pris Bertrand du Guesclin en un val,
> Les Poitevins près Lussac me défirent:
> A Mortemer mon corps enterrer firent.

His exquisite stall-plate still remains in his stall in St George's Chapel. And this reminds us that this idiosyncratic collection of memorials, extending over some six hundred years, forms 'such a storehouse of ancient and modern historical armory as exists nowhere else in Europe'. These plates reflect the history of their time: the early ones exquisite and small, with their coloured enamels; then the baroque flourish, sometimes in silver, of the seventeenth century; the late Victorian over-large and tasteless. During the odious Civil War the large silver plate of the Duke of Württemberg (Shakespeare's Count Mompelgart, Cousin Garmombles, of the *Merry Wives of Windsor*) 'gave so great a temptation that it was forced from the back of the stall whereto it was fixed'.

All this work of construction and remodelling took up much of the 1350's. The keep was garnished with a great clock, one of the earliest in England. There were bells for castle and chapel; the alabaster reredos for the latter required eighty horses to bring it from Nottingham. At last the virtual completion of the grand project was celebrated by a feast of extraordinary splendour, and solemn

The PORTRAICTVRES of King EDWARD the 3. with the first 25 KNIGHTS COMPANIOS in the HABIT of the ORDER and SVRCOATS of their ARMES.

Edward III and the first Knight
Companions of the Order of
the Garter.

religious ceremonies, on St George's day 1358. Henceforward St George, though he never existed, ousted as patron saint of England St Edward, who certainly had. As early as 1351 payments were made for twenty-four robes with mantles, embroidered with garters, and twelve standards for the Chapel – Queen and ladies received robes of the Order from the royal wardrobe. All was dedicated to St George; and still the celebrations continue, though no longer with masses and obits for the defunct, and with the religious side much diminished since the Reformation.

After Edward III's grand achievement nothing much was done to the Castle for the next century, though it was the scene of a number of events, some historic, some decisive, others pathetic or romantically appealing. In the autumn of 1361 the Black Prince and the beautiful widow, Joan of Kent, were married there; in the summer of 1369 his mother, Queen Philippa of Hainault and 'the burghers of Calais', died in the castle. In the spring of 1398 Richard II, seated on a platform in the upper ward, presided over the famous lists to decide the conflict between Bolingbroke and Mowbray – and disappointed everyone by banishing both. Here too Richard took his last leave of his child-wife, Isabel of France – wine and comfits in the Deanery – before his fatuous expedition to Ireland, which left the coast clear for Bolingbroke to return and take his throne.

As Henry IV, Bolingbroke was called to take the place of an incompetent, neurotic ruler by the will of the country, as far as it could be expressed, through Parliament and Church. But in the winter of his enthronement there was a conspiracy on the part of Richard's supporters, four earls abetted by the incorrigible bishop of Carlisle, to pounce upon Henry and his sons while spending the Christmas feast days at Windsor. One of the earls ratted and informed; Henry and his sons sped to London, where the citizens gave their support to the new and more promising monarch. The rebels invaded the Castle, but the birds had flown. This piece of foolery sealed poor Richard's fate at faraway Pontefract, and Henry kept Richard's young heir, the Earl of March, conveniently under surveillance at Windsor.

There he was succeeded, about 1413, by a more romantic figure, young James I of Scotland. This boy's elder brother had been murdered by one of those loving uncles of medieval history. James was being spirited away to France for safety and education, when he was captured in February 1406 at sea off Flamborough Head. A boy of twelve, he was confined in the Tower and other places. A valuable prize, he was well treated and his education provided for: instead of growing up a French poet, like Charles d'Orléans, he became an English poet, a follower of Chaucer (at one moment clerk of the works at Windsor).

In 1413, on account of plague in London, James was transferred hither, and here he met his amorous fate. For he tells us, in his poem *The King's Quair*, that it was in his eighteenth year that he first saw his bride walking in a garden under the walls in May.

> Now was there made, fast by the tower's wall,
>   A garden fair, and in the corners set
> An herbary green, with wandes long and small
>   Railèd about; and so with trees beset
>   Was all the place and hawthorn hedges knet,
> That there was none, walking the lawn forby,
> That might within scarce any wight espy.
>
> Eftsoons then cast I down mine eyes again
>   Whereas I saw, walking under the tower
> Full secretly, now come-in her to plain [play]
>   The fairest and the freshest younge flower
>   That ever I saw, methought, before that hour.
> For which suddenly abate, anon astart
> The blood of all my body to my heart.

No great matter as poetry, it is not bad for a king; and it reminds us that, oddly enough, Windsor Castle has made no such contribution to literature as emerged from the dank walls of the Tower of London – perhaps people were too happy and found other, more attractive things to do.

The little girl was Joan Beaufort, granddaughter of John of Gaunt, and there must have been opportunities of further meetings over the years until it proved a love-match, happily encouraged by all parties. In 1417 took place the visit of Henry v's ally, the Holy Roman Emperor himself, Sigismond. The multitude that came to see this unwonted spectacle overflowed into the lodgings of College and canons. Made a Knight of the Garter, the Emperor presented the Chapel with the most sacred of its relics: the heart of St George himself. Up to the later days of Henry VIII it used to be presented to the king to kiss and then to the Knights in turn: the Reformation ended that nonsense.

Not long after there was a plot on the part of the Lollard, Thomas Payne – one of those precursors of the Reformation – to rescue James and carry him off to Scotland. But the politic Henry v took him with him to France instead, to fight in his campaigns and rally the hostile Scots. After Henry's early death, his widow Catherine of France and the infant Henry VI were often at Windsor, company for James. And after the death of his wicked uncle, Albany, it was possible to return James to Scotland. As part of the deal he was to marry his Joan and 10,000 marks of his ransom were remitted as a wedding present. The

wedding took place in February 1424 at St Mary Overy (now Southwark cathedral), the banquet being given by the bride's uncle, Cardinal Beaufort, at Winchester House next door. The couple set off for Scotland, where they lived in conjugal bliss – until the time came for the King to be murdered, as so many Scots kings were, at the hands of a gang of nobles.

The next grand period in the beautification of Windsor was in the later decades of the fifteenth century, when the Yorkist Edward IV built the present St George's Chapel on a noble scale – we may surmise in rivalry with the Lancastrian Henry VI's chapel rising below in the meadows of Eton. In the intervening years – what with the long minority of Henry VI, the sequel to being driven out

Edward IV and Elizabeth Woodville, from a window in Canterbury
Cathedral. Edward built the present St George's Chapel at Windsor.

of France, the Wars of the Roses – little but repairs were effected at the Castle.
Even the Garter Feasts fell away; for years there was a very small attendance, the
foreign Knights not present, the Yorkists absented themselves, others had more
urgent affairs to attend to; in consequence for several years no elections were
made.

When young Edward IV won the throne by sheer military ability and went on
to prove himself capable of giving the country the good government poor
saintly Henry VI could not give it (he should have been a monk), a better period
set in for Windsor. Like James of Scotland Edward made a love-match, with
an amiable Lancastrian widow, Elizabeth Woodville. The young King and
Queen were much at Windsor; Edward enjoyed the hunting in the Forest, and

31

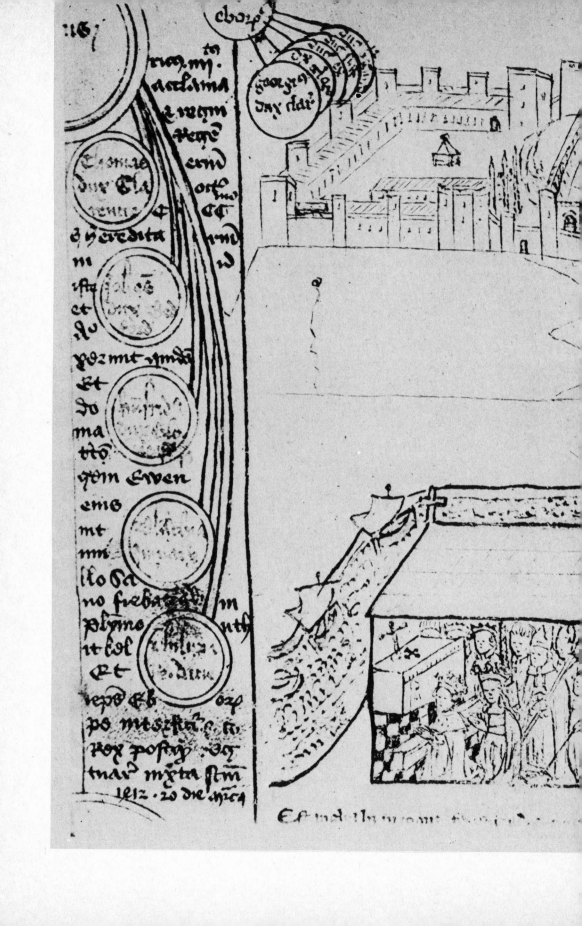

The earliest illustration of Windsor Castle (mid 15th century). In the foreground Henry VI and Queen Margaret pray before the altar.

Left: St George's Chapel, the north side of the sanctuary.
Right: The choir with the Sovereign's Stall.

Elizabeth gave birth to several of her children there. Handsome, outsize and very virile, it was no sinecure being married to Edward, who spread his favours around quite widely in addition. In these pursuits he had a boon-companion, Lord Hastings. So close was the companionship that Edward offered him a tomb beside his own in the splendid new chapel he was building, so that they might be together in death as in life.

Edward intended to enshrine himself and his new dynasty in a grander fane than the old chapel. He chose a site to the west of it, and to make room pulled down the hall and lodgings of the vicars-choral. If not so fine as Henry VI's

le dit Roi Edward apris suy le dit ...
du poeple du Roiat volunte put fizer
...

incomparable chapel at King's College, Cambridge, it is not far behind – a masterpiece of late Perpendicular architecture, shouting (rather than whispering) the last enchantments of the Middle Ages. It has a curious feature in being divided by transepts half-way down its length, no doubt to accommodate an unusually long choir for the Knights of the Garter. But its unbroken vista of vaulting is unsurpassed. There was to have been a central tower, apparently rectangular, not square, like Bath Abbey: a good thing it was not built, for it would have competed with the Round Tower in the roofscape.

While all this was a-building Edward's reign proceeded prosperously enough, with one break, in 1470–1 when his would-be mentor, Warwick the King-maker, turned against him and re-adopted poor broken Henry VI.

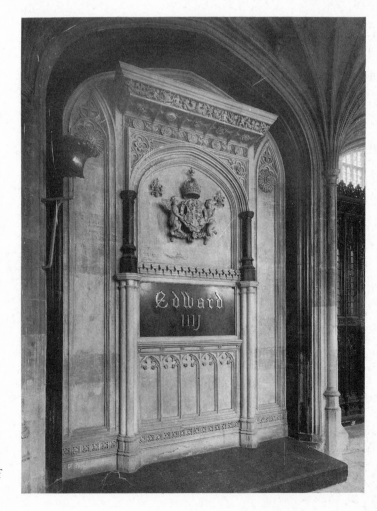

Right: Edward IV's tomb, St George's Chapel.

Left: Edward III delivers a Statute to Parliament. He was a great figure in Windsor history, and founded the Order of the Garter in 1348.

*Left, below & oppo-
site:* St George's
Chapel – Iron-work
by Master John
Tresillian.

This episode was ended at the field of Tewkesbury, where Henry's son and heir was killed by the Yorkists, and whence the indomitable Margaret of Anjou, defeated at last, was brought for several months' captivity at her own Windsor. (Such it was to have married a *roi fainéant*!)

Edward, now in complete control of his kingdom, was able to celebrate the Garter Feast next year, 1472, in special jollity. A large number of new Knights were recruited to fill up the diminished ranks of the Garter: the Duke of Norfolk, the Earl of Wiltshire, Lords Ferrers, Mountjoy and Howard. A stall was reserved for Edward's boy-prince – for whom a horrid fate was waiting all unknown in the Tower. Edward, an able ruler, was also (like his grandson Henry VIII) a good deal of a *faux-bonhomme*. At one time he would send a message to the mayor and aldermen of London – where he was always popular for his good government – inviting them to Windsor 'for none other errand but to have them hunt and be merry with him'. At another time he would promise to come and hunt with Archbishop Neville of York at his manor of the Moor, and when he arrived to prepare entertainment for the King, he found an order for his arrest instead. That was very like Henry VIII's turn of humour.

A Flemish envoy describes for us Edward's way of life at Windsor, in 1473. He was received by the inevitable Hastings and conducted to the suite of chambers set aside for him, hung with rich arras and occupied by grand beds of estate. After supper there was dancing and games with the ladies, Edward dancing with his little daughter Elizabeth, afterwards (after what happenings!) the wife of the respectable Henry VII. Next day the envoy was presented to the child Prince Edward – so briefly Edward V – while the King took him over his garden and into the vineyard on the southern slope.

Edward's mistake was not to live long enough to see his boys grow safely to maturity. He himself had disposed of his brother, Clarence, by consigning him to a butt of malmsey in the Tower. That left only one brother, Gloucester, to look after the well-being of the house of York. Edward was already preparing his tomb in the place of honour on the north side of the choir – it was never finished, and Hastings' tomb remained empty. But a great artist and craftsman in ironwork, a Cornishman, John Tresillian, wrought magnificent gates, with towers in the Perpendicular style, to separate the tomb from the aisle. Everyone regards these gates as 'without doubt the most remarkable work of their period in that material remaining in the country'. In addition the Chapel contains a large number of decorative locks and iron fittings – memorials to an artist far more worthy of respect than the fighting fools and political disputants of the age who figure more largely there.

On the opposite side of the choir was the shrine of Sir John Shorn, a figure of medieval folklore – 'Master Shorn's Tower' still exists. He was a Buckinghamshire magician:

> Sir John Shorn, gentleman born,
> Conjured the Devil into a boot.

The canons of Windsor, avid for relics – and the offerings of the faithful that went with them – procured his bones from their resting-place at North Marston and set them up to be venerated here. When the Reformation turfed them out, the Canons complained that this had lost them £500 a year. Perhaps this was a pardonable exaggeration – at any rate, a good deal of waste was saved: such is popular idiocy.

Edward died in April 1483; his brother summarily executed the booncompanion, Hastings, in June, without trial of any sort. After that there was no turning back. In the same month Richard seized his nephew's throne; the two boys were never seen alive again after that August. Richard was briefly at Windsor on his way to Warwick, whence the order for their murder was sent. The country turned against the murderer; that autumn his brother-in-law, St Leger, revolted against him and was executed – there is a plaque in the Chapel to his wife, Richard's sister, Duchess of Exeter. In April 1484 Richard's only son and heir died, and in March next year his wife. Richard was alone with his remorse. He brought the body of Henry VI – who had been done to death in the Tower on a night when we know Richard was there – to be buried honourably at last in St George's Chapel.

All was to no avail. Retribution was awaiting him at Bosworth Field in August 1485 – where no-one would fight for him except his little gang of cronies – just two agonising years after the murder of his nephews.

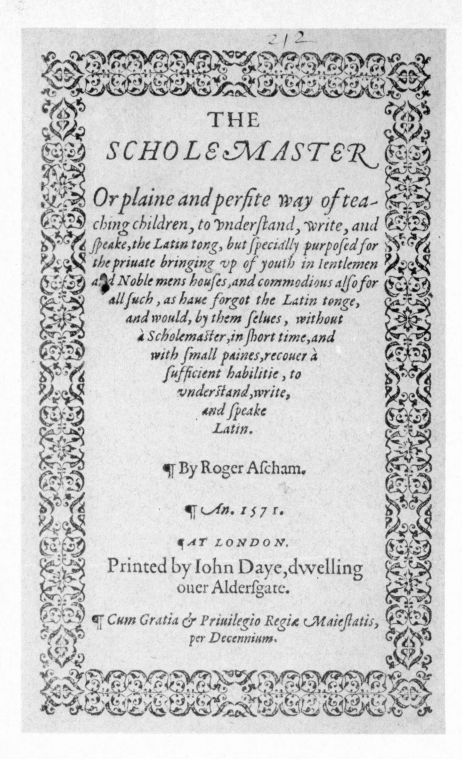

Frontispiece from Roger Ascham's *The Schoolmaster* – 'a prime
contribution of Windsor to literature'.

2

Tudor Historic Decisions

URING Richard III's usurpation no elections to the Garter were made – not unnaturally, for he had other things on his mind. But with the return to stability and respectability under Henry VII things resumed their normal course. In 1488 the new king gave a grand Garter feast at Windsor in the great hall, attended by all the Knights and canons. As also by young Elizabeth of York, now his queen, and by his famous mother, the Lady Margaret, through whom his claim to the throne came.

A stable reign enabled Henry VII to accomplish a great deal. At Windsor he finished his father-in-law, Edward IV's Chapel, completing the roof, and he rebuilt the framework of Henry III and Edward III's chapel to the east of it, intending to make it a shrine for the saintly Henry VI. Offerings were already being made at his tomb – St George's still possesses an iron alms-box for them. But the process for Henry's canonisation never went through – though a much better man than some who got over the hurdles. This smaller chapel remained unfinished and empty, to have a curiously variegated future.

For his own comfort and his queen's Henry added to the royal lodgings an attractive habitation in the form of a three-storeyed tower. This has been subsequently altered by Wyatville, but originally it had two very decorative oriel windows running up the height of the upper storeys. This proved very convenient for the grand entertainments of 1506, towards the end of Henry's successful reign.

The visitors of 31 January to 14 February had not been expected: they proved providential flotsam and jetsam thrown up on the coast of Dorset by storm in the Channel. These were the young parents of the Emperor Charles V – the handsome Philip of Habsburg and his wife Juana la Loca, so besotted on him that she carried his coffin around with her for long after his early death. She was the sister of Catherine of Aragon, who had been married to Henry's son, Arthur, and subsequently to Henry VIII, by whom she had Queen Mary I. All those three women had a stubborn fixedness of mind in common, a fanatic Spanish character.

Philip and Juana's fleet had been dispersed and themselves forced to take refuge at Weymouth. Here a local youth, John Russell, who had learned to speak French in the Channel trade, was sent for to interpret for them and accompany them to Windsor: it made his fortune and that of the Russells ever after. The canny Henry VII had every intention of making the most of this uncovenanted mercy: he laid on courtly entertainment, the politest welcome, by way of extracting a too favourable commercial treaty with the Netherlands, when Philip was in no condition to resist.

Assembling all the notables of the kingdom he could muster to impress his guest and victim, Henry rode out a mile from the Castle – an unwonted honour – to meet Philip by the way in an arable field. After many salutations, attended by their retinue, the Earl of Derby bearing the sword of state, the two kings entered the Castle, the minstrels and sackbuts playing at the gate. The grand chambers in the new tower were assigned to Philip, a suite of three rooms hung with arras, equipped with beds of estate – a fourth was hung with cloth of gold, crimson velvet arms and devices. There ensued a round of entertainments, ceremonies, services in public; in private Henry got down to the real business – extracting the best terms possible for English trade while giving as little as possible in return. Thus was shaped what the Netherlanders called the *Intercursus Malus* – most favoured nation terms for English goods, with no reciprocity.

We are fortunate, when so much is impersonal about the first Tudor king, a prime man of business, to have an appealing personal description of this historic visit. January 31 being 'fasting day and Our Lady Even', each king dined in his own chamber; but 'after supper was done the king of Castile took with him but one torch and five or six gentlemen, and privily went to visit the king'. (French was Henry's second language; he did his serious reading mostly in French.)

Next day, Sunday, they went in state together to High Mass in St George's, sung by the bishop of Chichester *in pontificalibus*. Afterwards we have a glimpse of the two kings – one elderly and worn, whom the younger affected to treat as father – standing by the fire together in Philip's dining-chamber. That evening he went to visit the ladies, the young widow Catherine and Henry's buxom daughter Mary, who was to dance the elderly Louis XII (Charles d'Orléans' son) into his grave. The young ladies danced and played on the lute and claregals (virginals), while the kings talked business: there was plenty to discuss.

February 2 being Candlemas Day, the candles were hallowed by the archbishop of Canterbury, the kings going in procession around the hall with their tapers. Then Mass, followed by a sermon in French. The following days the treaty was hammered out between the respective councils, with intervals for

The wrought iron alms box in St George's Chapel.

hunting the deer in the park, baiting a horse in the courtyard while the kings looked on from the new tower. On 9 February Philip was invested with the Garter. We have a full description of the ceremonies, in which the relic of the True Cross – there were enough relics of it all over Europe to build a house – played a part, with two tapers burning beside it for its honour. More important, the treaty of trade and amity, duly signed and sealed by both parties, was sworn to on the gospels. A Te Deum of thanksgiving was sung in honour of the agreement reached.

Prince Henry was awarded the Golden Fleece, as he was later to be awarded Catherine of Aragon, rather than return her dowry. On 10 February Queen Juana at length arrived with her servants. 'They entered by the little park, and so secretly came by the backside of the castle unto the king's new tower, where at the stairfoot the king met with her, and kissed and embraced her.' Four days later Philip left for Richmond, 'hawking and hunting by the way as he rode' – it was all open country then; while Juana was carried in Elizabeth of York's litter to Plymouth to embark for Spain. Not until St George's day did Philip set sail to follow his loving wife to an early death.

And the treaty, the secret Treaty of Windsor?

Henry gained the surrender of the de la Pole 'White Rose', Richard III's nephew, who was consigned to the Tower, where he lived safe and sound so long as Henry lived. When Henry VIII succeeded, who inherited the Yorkist proclivities of his grandfather Edward IV, he sent his cousin to the block. As for the commercial treaty, in spite of its having been sworn on the gospels, it was never confirmed or put into operation. The business-man king had over-reached himself.

That November there was another historic reception at Windsor, of a far more interesting man than Philip: Baldassare Castiglione, author of *The Courtier*, the book that set the ideal pattern of courtly education and culture for every country in Renaissance Europe. Castiglione had come to receive the Garter as proxy for the Duke of Urbino, bringing as a present the famous picture of St George by the young Raphael. Henry received the ambassador at Greenwich, but did not accompany him along 'the fair causeway' he had lately made between London and Windsor.

Castiglione was entertained by the Dean, Christopher Urswick, in the Deanery he had re-built. Urswick, an early supporter of Henry in exile, was a cultivated scholar and generous friend of Erasmus, who dedicated to him his 'Lucian's Dream'. Next day followed the usual ceremonies of installation, Castiglione taking the vows on behalf of the Duke. The fees for the honour were very heavy, but in the case of foreign princes they were paid by the Sovereign – everything was at his expense. All the 'Courtier' had to do was to bestow a gratuity on the College, and receive presents of a gold collar, horses and dogs from Henry, who knew how to be sumptuous when it was politic.

Next year Philip of Habsburg died; his banners were offered up on the altar where he had taken the oaths of the Order. Two years more and Henry was dead, bequeathing in his will a large gilt image of St George to the College, to be placed on the altar on Feast-days.

Henry VIII was much attached to Windsor: his shade looms large over the place and in its folklore. He built the main gate into the Castle, and is buried there with his favourite Queen, Jane Seymour, while his father lies in Westminster. One doesn't think of the secret and taciturn father, to whom the Tudors owed everything, so much as of the extrovert son, a big bully of a man who turned after his Yorkist grandfather, addicted to out-of-door and martial sports, overlarge and running to fat, with more than an eye for women, capricious and cruel – and always popular (which his father never was).

The new reign opened in great jollity and Henry enjoyed himself hugely for years – until he found himself caught in revolutionary currents and forced to take control. Fortunately for the country he was well capable. In early years he was Prince Charming; at Windsor we hear of him 'exercising himself daily in shooting, singing, dancing, wrestling, casting of the bar, playing at the recorders, flute, virginals, in setting of songs and making of ballads. He did set two full Masses, every one of them with five parts, which were sung oftentimes in his chapels.' Flattery of royal persons and flummery apart, Henry was a capable musician and a composer whose music is still performed in choirs and places where they sing. From the Windsor Accounts we can see how life was in these charming years. Offerings to St George and 'good King Harry' every time the young king came and went; gratuities to the schoolmaster and children at Eton; a large payment 'to a stranger from beyond the sea for a goodly instrument'. 'To Cornish, Master of the Children of the Chapel, for singing of *Audivi* on All Hallows' day, 20s; for Nicholas Bishop [i.e. the Boy Bishop], 10 marks; for singing *Gloria in Excelsis* on Christmas day, 40s. To the Lord of Misrule, 20 marks.' There are the wages of the Master of the King's Barge, of Lord Antony for his spearmen, payments for bringing guardjackets from the Tower; rewards to messengers from the king of France.

Coming events cast their shadows before. In 1510 the Lady Margaret's confessor, Dr Fisher, brought the hallowed Golden Rose from the Pope, and received £100 in gold for it. In 1515 Henry wrote to Leo X that nothing had given him so much pleasure in his life as Wolsey's election as Cardinal. Next year two foreigners arrived at the Castle with 'as great a desire as souls in Purgatory' to see King and Cardinal, but just missed them.

In these early years of enjoyment of life Henry was content to leave the business of the state to the Cardinal with his inordinate appetite for work – and everything else. There is in fact an extraordinary letter from Wolsey, his first extant letter, written at Windsor to his patron, Bishop Foxe, when he was still no more than the King's almoner, which already bespeaks his overweening ambition and arrogance. He tells Foxe that the Howard Earl of Surrey had met with a cool reception at Court and had gone home in high dudgeon. He suggested that, with a little push, Surrey might be 'utterly excluded . . . whereof in my poor judgment no little good should ensue.' Not bad for a 'humble priest', the butcher's son, in regard to a Lord Treasurer on his way to the dukedom of Norfolk. (The Dukes, however, had the last word.)

The Garter Feasts were kept up with greater ostentation and extravagance by a young monarch who enjoyed spending what his careful father had saved. In May 1519 the crowd of people, courtiers and nobles, who rode down with Henry was so great that their retinues had to be restricted according to rank: sixty horsemen for a duke, fifty for a marquis, and so on, 'in consideration of a scarcity and straitness of lodgings, as well as in avoiding and eschewing of the corrupt air'. Henry often took refuge at Windsor when the plague was hot in London; we find him there in the bad plague-summer of 1517, with his physician, Dionysius Memo, and three favourite gentlemen – no-one admitted to spread the disease. Wolsey, who had been ill several times, had gone on pilgrimage to the shrine of Walsingham.

On the Emperor Charles v's visit in 1522, after the hollow but spendthrift farce of Henry's Field of the Cloth of Gold with his rival Francis I, Charles came down to Windsor for the serious business of getting the English alliance. His installation as Knight of the Garter was part of the proceedings for the benefit of the public – 'conspicuous consumption'. The real affair was another Treaty of Windsor, by which the Emperor engaged himself to marry his little cousin, Catherine of Aragon's daughter, the Princess Mary. He had no intention of abiding by his engagement, of course; he wanted Henry's alliance to serve his turn and, when it ceased to do so, he repudiated her. Wolsey had pushed his powers as Papal Legate to the extreme to constitute a court to hold the contracting parties to their signed and sealed engagement, under pain of ecclesiastical censure. But who cared for that – orthodox Emperor any more than schismatic King, when it suited them?

Catherine's inability to provide any other than a sickly daughter to assure the succession to the throne made her future doubtful, while Henry's passion for Anne Boleyn – who insisted on marriage – sealed Catherine's fate. Henry had proved his ability to sire male offspring with his natural son by Bessie Blount, Henry Fitzroy, whom he created Duke of Richmond. Born in 1519 the boy

'At Windsor we hear of him exercising himself daily in shooting, singing, dancing, wrestling, casting of the bar, playing at the recorders, flute, virginals, in setting of scenes and making of ballads.' *Right:* The score for Henry VIII's song *Pastance with Good Company.*

grew up at Windsor, where he lived a great deal in the company of Norfolk's son, Surrey, a couple of years older. This brilliant and arrogant youth became the first poet of the time, introducing the influence of Italian Renaissance poetry.

In one of his later poems, 'Prisoned in Windsor, He Recounteth his Pleasure there Passed', he recalls those blissful days:

> So cruel prison how could betide, alas,
> As proud Windsor, where I in lust and joy
> With a king's son my childish years did pass
> In greater joys than Priam's sons of Troy.

Henry Howard, Earl of Surrey, painting by Guillim Scrots, 1546.

> Where each sweet place returns a taste full sour:
> The large green courts where we were wont to hove,
> With eyes cast up into the maidens' tower
> And easy sighs such as folk draw in love.

He goes on to remember:

> The stately seats, the ladies bright of hue,
> The dances short, long tales of great delight,

the games they played, tennis in the new court Henry VII had built and where Philip of Habsburg had played. When they missed the ball they would look up to see their dame keeping an eye on them from the leads above. Then there was training for the tilt:

> The gravelled ground, with sleeves tied on the helm,
> On foaming horse with swords and friendly hearts,
> With cheer, as though one should another whelm,
> Where we have fought and chasèd oft with darts.
> With silver drops the mead yet spread for ruth,
> In active games of nimbleness and strength
> Where we did strain, trainèd with swarms of youth,
> Our tender limbs that yet shot up in length.

Beyond were all the pleasures of park and forest, holt and hurst, the chase, the merry cry of hounds. Even on winter nights within the walls, there were

> The secret thoughts, imparted with such trust,
> The wanton talk, the divers change of play,
> The friendship sworn, each promise kept so just,
> Wherewith we passed the winter night away.

Alas for the promises of youth, the trusting friendship – as Henry's reign wore on, all turned sour: his boy Richmond died, and Surrey, ruined by mad pride – though Henry bore with his caprices surprisingly patiently – ended on a block in the Tower.

Henry had to beget a legitimate male heir – this was his problem, which the country understood very well. He left Windsor in July 1531 in the company of Anne, without saying goodbye to the Queen. In August she was ordered to leave the Castle. In September next year Anne was created Marchioness of Pembroke 'in the chamber of salutation they call the Presence', approved by the French ambassador – politics, of course: a snub for Catherine's nephew, the Emperor. Henry was remarkably patient, caught between these two determined and stubborn women (Catherine should have given up and gone into a nunnery). Not until January 1533 were Henry and Anne secretly married; in September Elizabeth was born – if she had been a boy, all might have been well. (In the event it turned out better.)

In 1536 came the crisis of Henry's reign. At the end of January Anne was delivered of a son – dead. But at the beginning of the month Catherine had died. So Henry could now make a clearance, and begin again. He was already in love with pale, innocent Jane Seymour. On 19 May Queen Anne was executed in the Tower – whether guilty or no of the charges, she had led a dangerous tiger of a man a dreadful dance. On 30 May Henry married Jane.

That autumn there broke out in Lincolnshire the rebellion known as the Pilgrimage of Grace. It was followed by a still larger rising in Yorkshire, with reverberations all over the North. Some forty thousand men were in arms against the King and the new deal imposed by the progressive South – and there were no standing forces to deal with such an army of insurgents. What made it so dangerous was that it was not just a mob of the people, it was led by their natural leaders the gentry, inspired by their clergy, particularly dispossessed abbots and monks, and it had the covert sympathy of conservative peers. Behind it were the views of the old Catholic aristocrats, Courtenays and Poles, and behind that there was the threat of foreign intervention, Emperor and Pope. It all made a most formidable combination; Henry was taken by surprise, he was for once alarmed – and no less furious.

He shut himself up that autumn at Windsor, whence he took control of the situation, so far as he could, in his own hands. Now we see what he was like in action: giving all the orders himself, dispatching contingents as fast as he could raise them to the North. He could not be sure of his own instruments – Norfolk and others: they were encouraged by the promises of a disingenuous politician. He set himself to drive a wedge between the leaders of the movement and the people, who were less trustful; in this he ultimately succeeded. He was forced to temporise, which redoubled his anger at this demonstration from the backward northern counties, 'Yea, and that the beastliest [Yorkshire] in the whole realm.' He was forced to put his case – still more humiliating; the propaganda, directed by him, went out. He circularised the bishops, urging them to stand fast, reminding them who had appointed them to their sees and fat revenues. Reassuring the rebels, with no intention of abiding by his assurances, dividing them, seducing the doubtful by *fausse bonhommie* and promises, frightening the craven – he ultimately won through. It was a hardened man who emerged from the crisis; when the rebellion, which had been fended off by November, tried to renew itself in the spring, Henry took an almighty revenge in the North.

What was at stake was the future of the new deal. This had the progressive, expansive dynamic of the South behind it – especially London, the towns, the governing elements in the counties. The strength of Henry's case was that every step in the rejection of Papal jurisdiction, the assumption of a national English Church, the suppression of the monasteries, had been carried forward by the will of the nation as expressed in Parliament. The forward course was not to be held up by backward-looking elements in the backward North, nor by conservatives among the old aristocracy.

And, as is the way with idiotic mob-movements of this kind, it cleared the way for speeding up the new deal, enabled Henry to go on to suppress the greater monasteries, and to deal savagely with aristocratic opponents now left dangerously exposed. In terms of *real-politik* that is all the Pilgrimage of Grace achieved, with its banners of the Five Wounds, its priors and abbots who survived to be strung up as traitors.

As it happens, we have a vivid close-up of Henry in action, as so rarely, showing us just what he was like, in the letters written from Windsor that autumn. Sir Ralph Sadler reported to Cromwell in London, where Henry kept him to raise money and munitions for the forces going north, that the King read his letters thoroughly 'and bade me keep them till he had supped. In his going to the Queen's chamber to supper, I told him by the way, you had written me that the Father [Abbot] of Sion was departed.' This reminded Henry that 'the Charterhouse in London is not ordered as I would have it' – the monks had been obstinate – and that he had commanded Cromwell long ago to put the monks out of the house. Cromwell had been too lenient and written that they had submitted; but Henry would not accept their obedience, 'seeing that they had been so long obstinate'. We see that Cromwell, who had to take all the blame for the Suppression had a harsher driver behind him. 'By this his Grace was in the Queen's chamber, ready to wash and sit down to supper.'

After supper, he returned to his own chamber for more business. There was Queen Jane's coronation to consider; plague in Westminster, even in the Abbey, put him in doubt whether to defer it. He would summon the Council immediately, and Cromwell was to come to Windsor. Sadler said that Cromwell would not get word till tomorrow afternoon and next day was Michaelmas Day. ' "What then?" said his Grace, "Michaelmas Day is not so high a day".' So Cromwell was to come on Michaelmas Day, convenient or not. 'Windsor, 27 September, at 12 a clock of the night, which is our accustomed hour in the Court to go to bed.'

In mid-October the Lincolnshire rising was receding; Henry wrote detailed instructions to the Duke of Suffolk how he was to deal with the rebels. By 'one means or another' he was to get hold of Lincoln, camp in the Close 'with an eye to the country round about so that no man stir again but he be straight had by the head and hanged'. But now news came that 'the greater part of Yorkshire be up and the whole country to favour their opinions – the same that were reported in Lincolnshire. This matter hangeth yet like a fever, one day good, another bad.' Henry was alarmed by this new and larger movement; 'his Majesty appeareth to fear much this matter, and has no great trust in Darcy'. (This peer paid for his connivance with the insurgents with his head.)

Here was the nub of the matter. Henry did not know whom he could wholly trust among the commanders he sent against the rebels – Norfolk or Exeter, for example. He thought of leading an army north in person; then thought better of it – that would leave the coast clear for the opposition nobles in case of accidents in the field. Better to remain at the centre directing events – and he had the excuse that a son was on the way. He sent out the news as good propaganda, along with a hundred leaflets justifying his course as agreed on by Council and Parliament.

Furious at having to argue his case with fools, Henry wrote to Cromwell, raising money in the City, that he was 'to taste the fat priests thereabouts' – naming some of the rich prebendaries of St Paul's. Though regarding himself as a good Catholic, he had no more illusions about clerics than he had about anybody else, and was decidedly anti-clerical. We have an example of his ruthless humour when we remember that the Earl of Wiltshire was Anne Boleyn's father. The King was glad 'you [Cromwell] remembered my lord of Wiltshire and that you wrote for so good a sum. For his Grace, being merry, said there was a servant of King Edward's, his grandfather, which once made a suit unto him for 1000 oaks that he might only obtain twenty. So he trusted your request to my lord of Wiltshire should purchase £500 or such a matter, by the reason it was so great: which, being less, would else percase have wrought nothing with him.' So much for a relegated father-in-law.

Henry was determined to get Aske, leader of the Yorkshire insurgents, into his hands. From Windsor Norfolk wrote to the dubious Darcy, 'to declare yourself, I advise you to take, alive or dead, but alive if possible, that arrant traitor Aske, which will extinct the ill bruit and raise you in the favour of his Highness'. But he did not – and so lost that precarious quality, Henry's favour. Norfolk wrote again, 'I beg you will put away suspicion and induce others to unite with me. I have lived too long to think otherwise than truly and honestly.' He repeated this in another appeal, adding 'and when I do otherwise may God take my life'. When Norfolk left Windsor for the North, Henry wrote to him 'whereas you desire us, in case of any mischance, to be good lord to your children, although we trust no such thing shall happen, yet we assure you that in such case we shall not fail to remember your children, being your lively images, with our princely favour'.

Well, we remember what happened to Surrey, and reflect what reptiles they were.

Meanwhile Henry was writing, at midnight on 28 October, to the Earl of Derby to keep Lancashire in line. 'If on your coming to Whalley you find the abbot and monks restored again [they had optimistically gone back to their rookery], you shall at once cause the abbot and certain of the monks to be hanged on long pieces of timber or otherwise out of the steeple, and the rest to be executed in such places as you think fit. Putting the remainder of the people in no doubt of our mercy; but passing it over as though you took none else for offenders but the ringleaders, whom you cause to be presented to you by, as it were for their excuses. You must have special regard to the apprehension of all such captains. Let none escape.'

Such was Henry's temper, not Cromwell's. In the letters from Windsor that autumn we can look into Henry's very mind. Like his grandfather, Edward IV, he was well equipped to rule humans.

And poor Queen Jane? Life with her must have been restful after the pious, unmovable obstinacy of Catherine and the hysterical tantrums of Anne. Jane was a good girl: nothing but good is known of her. She passed silently through the world, leaving few traces of herself. Here is one, a brief message to Cromwell that November urging a good deed on behalf of someone in trouble: 'ye could not do a better deed for the increase of your eternal reward in the world to come. At my lord's castle of Windsor.' In that humble ascription we glimpse something of her submission to her fate.

On 12 October next year, at Hampton Court she gave birth to the so long desired son, Edward; twelve days later she was dead.

Henry genuinely loved her, after his fashion; she was the only one of his wives whom he mourned, and in his will he desired to be laid in the grave by her side. Her funeral at Windsor was attended by Catherine's daughter, the Lady Mary, as chief mourner, and she remained there with her father to keep him company right up to New Year.

Henry had intended to make over his father's eastern chapel as a mausoleum for himself. In the days of the Cardinal's glory – and his own more generous youth – he had handed it over to Wolsey for his resting-place. Wolsey was a man of Renaissance tastes, and he called in Benedetto da Rovezzano to design a splendid tomb. From the grand sculpted candlesticks that exist we can imagine something like the chapel of the Catholic Kings, Ferdinand and Isabella, in the cathedral of Granada, with the great taper burning eternally between them.

At the time of Wolsey's fall the tomb was unfinished; in the hideous days of the Commonwealth the precious metals and enamels were sold away, two of the splendid candlesticks are at St Bavon in Ghent. The coffin-chest was taken later to bury Nelson in, in the crypt of St Paul's.

Henry's will re-established thirteen Poor Knights on a firmer propertied foundation, and ordained that he be buried in St George's. In the cold February of 1547 his gross carcass was borne down to Windsor in a chariot, the funeral procession stretching four miles. In the Chapel a hearse of no less than thirteen storeys, with hundreds of candles, was erected for him – we can see what it looked like from a fine Gothic drawing of the hearse of one of the last abbots of Westminster. Everything about him was outsize.

The Reformation made marked changes at Windsor as elsewhere. Henry's convictions had been Catholic, but the arrangements of his will, the Council with whom he surrounded his boy as king, gave the Reformation impulse its head, and it leaped forward. He was too good a politician not to recognise that its advance was inevitable. He had left money for daily Masses to be said for him at the altar by his tomb 'while the world should endure'. The provision lasted for a year. During his reign every deceased Knight of the Garter had 1000 Masses said for him at the King's expense. The Reformation eliminated this waste.

The year 1548 saw a considerable simplification of Garter ceremonies, and a conference of bishops and theologians adjourned to Windsor 'to prepare a uniform order of prayer'. Archbishop Cranmer, the best liturgical scholar of them all, had the greatest difficulty in getting the bishops into line. Some of them favoured Transubstantiation, whatever that might mean – though they had been prepared to burn folks for it. During the Catholic reaction in the early forties, a hot-headed Canon of Windsor brought charges of heresy against four servants of the Court there; three of the poor fellows were burned, the fourth, John Marbeck, was saved only by powerful friends. He would have been a great loss, for he was the accomplished musician who set the whole Prayer Book, when ready, to plainchant.

Others of the Commission doubted if Transubstantiation meant anything at all – like many of their successors in the Apostolic Succession today. However, the first Prayer Book managed to get agreed in 1549, and young Edward was able to urge upon his obstinate sister Mary that it had the support of the clergy in Convocation. (That had no more authority with her than with her father.)

In this year too the annual Feast of the Garter at Windsor was discontinued; it might be held anywhere the Sovereign happened to be, and the Statutes of the Order were to be reformed. St George was demoted – it was simply to be known as the Order of the Garter – and his image displaced from the altar. The cross in its coat-of-arms might be kept, 'because it was not the special ensign of St George, and it is a mere fable that he ever bore it'. If they had only known that the Pope in time would declare it a mere fable that he ever existed! – but it has taken four hundred years to reach that rational conclusion.

The young King, a convinced Protestant, was anxious 'to purge the Order of all papistical and superstitious practices', while maintaining it for chivalric and charitable purposes. Among the latter he proposed to divert its revenues to 'the maintenance of scholars at the universities, the amendment of highways and making banks upon rivers; and on the demise of the existing canons and choristers, their incomes were to be diverted to the pay of itinerant preachers'. That was regarded as somehow more educational. The Edwardians considered that it was the serpent Satan who had 'craftily stuffed the Statutes of this fellow-ship with many doubtful, superstitious and repugnant opinions'; and they defended dropping St George, 'lest the honour which is only due unto God should be thereby abused'.

However, the Statutes had only just been purged and cleansed when Edward died and Mary shortly restored her father's, as part of her determination to have things once more as they had ceased to be.

One cannot make changes in men's beliefs, the subliminal area in what they are pleased to call their minds, without heads getting broken. In reaction against the new Prayer Book a swarm of benighted peasants, instigated by their priests, in the more backward parts of central Devon and west Cornwall – the parishes around Sampford Courtenay and the Lizard area – broke out in rebellion. This, along with an even more serious social rising in Norfolk and disturbances against enclosure in the Midlands, put Protector Somerset's rule (Edward's uncle) in jeopardy. His combination of arrogant superiority towards his equals with liberal-mindedness towards the people was not a good recipe for holding power in revolutionary times. A coalition was formed within the Council which turned the majority against him. Warwick, on his way to becoming Duke of Northumberland, formed an alliance between the left-wing Protestants and Catholic conservatives like Southampton. Northumberland's own convictions, such as they were, were rather Catholic than Protestant; he eventually cheated the Catholic wing of the coalition, realising that the tide was with Protestants. (It is not generally known that the conservative Southampton moved over with the flowing tide before, shortly, he died.)

In these decisive events Windsor provided the scene once more.

When the crisis blew up Somerset was with the King at Hampton Court.

Overleaf: The Poor Knights' lodgings built by Queen Mary.

Realising that it was indefensible, the Protector woke the King out of his bed on an October night and hurried him off, with Cranmer, Paget, and his own supporters, to Windsor. The delicate boy caught a chill; he did not forgive his uncongenial uncle that frightening ride through the night to Windsor. He entered in his Diary, coldly, impassively, as usual: 'that night, with all the people, at 9 or 10 o'clock at night, I went to Windsor, and there was watch and ward kept every night.' He did not like the Castle: 'Methinks I am in prison: here be no galleries nor gardens to walk in.'

Somerset thought of resisting and began levying archers in the neighbourhood. But the majority of the Council were in control in London and soon got possession of the Tower. The Protector hoped for the support of Russell and Herbert returning with their army from putting down the rebellion in the West. But they declared for their brethren of the Council, and Somerset saw that he must yield. Sir Philip Hoby – whom we see on his Renaissance tomb at nearby Bisham – handled the negotiations with such skill that, after a week and a meeting of the full Council at Windsor upon which Somerset was arrested and put under a strong guard, he was bundled safely off to the Tower.

The Reformation dynamic could now go forward with gathering speed. In July 1550 the Council sent down its orders to the College and town to deface their altars out of hand. Feathering their own nests as fast as they could, they left the state without funds for its needs. They ordered the Dean and Chapter to hand over some £800 of the lands left by Henry for the Poor Knights, 'because the disposition of these lands is not yet appointed'. It was not appointed till the charitably inclined Mary – except where religious convictions were concerned – came to the throne and confirmed them in accordance with her father's will.

However, the Council did one good deed for the Castle: they ordered a great conduit to be made to bring a sufficient water supply to it. Characteristically the stone used was that intended for building up the front of the choir, presumably the unfinished eastern chapel. The lead was to come from Reading and Woburn abbeys. Even when Queen Mary settled Henry's thirteen Poor Knights in the lodgings she built for them west of her father's gateway, the building stone came from Reading Abbey.

With Elizabeth's reign a rather more civilised era opened; true, there were plague and war, but Mary's burnings came to an end. During the severe plague the troops brought back from France in 1563, the Queen spent the autumn and winter at Windsor. She spent a good deal of time studying with her tutor, Roger Ascham, who wrote that 'beside her perfect readiness in Latin, Italian, French and Spanish, she readeth here now at Windsor more Greek every day than some prebendaries of this church doth read Latin in a whole week'. No doubt true enough of ordinary mortals. For recreation there was hunting with Leicester in the Forest; the Queen killed a great fat stag, which she had sent to her archbishop, 'parboiled ... because the weather was hot and the deer somewhat chafed.'

It was during this winter that there took shape one of the first important English books devoted to the subject of education and teaching. This was Ascham's *The Schoolmaster*, dedicated to the Queen, a prime contribution of Windsor to literature. Ascham tells us how it originated. Sir William Cecil, now Secretary, never talked business at table; he liked to have intelligent company around him who would talk about books – he was rather donnish in his tastes. One day he had at his table Sir William Petre, a benefactor to Exeter College, and Sir John Mason of All Souls, former Secretaries; Dean Wotton of Canterbury, really a diplomatist; Sir Walter Mildmay, who later founded Emmanuel College, Sir Richard Sackville and Mr Haddon, all of the Exchequer, the last the leading Latinist of the time; and a couple more with Ascham.

Cecil began the discourse with the news that several scholars had run away from Eton that morning, for fear of beating. Beating was the regular thing in Elizabethan schools, but the highly civilised Cecil did not approve of it. He wished that schoolmasters had more discretion and considered that many of them punished 'rather the weakness of nature than the fault of the scholar'. This was apt to discourage scholars and make them hate learning before they knew what it meant and what it could do for them, whereby many forsook their book and would rather do anything else for a living.

This started the discussion. Petre, somewhat severe in nature, favoured the rod to keep the school in order and thus give scholars a better chance to learn. Dean Wotton was a mild man, and thought school should be a place of play and pleasure, not of fear and bondage. Walter Haddon of King's agreed with Petre and thought that the best schoolmaster of the age was the greatest beater – this was Nicholas Udall of Eton, whose interest in his boys was not confined to beating, though that may have stimulated it. Mason, a Fellow of All Souls who had risen from the people, laughed at both sides and poked fun at both naughty boys and 'lewd schoolmasters'.

Sir Richard Sackville – who made the fortunes of the house of Knole – contributed nothing to the discussion, but was evidently impressed and thinking it over. After dinner Ascham went up to read Demosthenes with the Queen – her rooms were at the top of Henry VII's tower. Sackville came up later and, taking Ascham by the hand to the oriel window, he said he wouldn't have missed the discussion at dinner for a good deal of money – a great compliment from him, whom the jealous called 'Fill-Sack' for the money he was making.

Elizabeth I in the Garter Procession, from Gerard's *Proceeding of Sovereigns and Knight Companions of the Order of the Garter at St George's Feast*, 1578.

He confessed that he had been so sorely beaten by his own schoolmaster in his youth that he had been put off learning – and how much he regretted it now. He besought Ascham to undertake the tutoring of his clever grandson, Robert, (who became a notable scholar in consequence) and, more, to write down his thoughts on the whole subject.

Such was the Windsor origin of this English classic, still alive because of its personal inflexion, its reminiscences of the education of Elizabeth and Lady Jane Grey, whose tutor Ascham had been, of the new Renaissance teaching of Greek at Cambridge by Sir John Cheke, Edward VI's tutor, of Erasmus and du Bellay, and much else of interest.

Elizabeth I was more attached to Windsor than is generally realised – one associates her more with Greenwich, where she was born, Richmond, where she died, Whitehall or Nonsuch. Hampton Court she did not like; she had smallpox there and thought it unhealthy. In fact she spent more money on renovation and building at Windsor than on any of her other palaces. We can still see something of her work in the gallery she built between her grandfather's tower and the gate to the upper ward: this is now used, if that is the word for it, as the Royal Library. Much of the rest of her work has disappeared: the charming private chapel she reconstructed, the Rubbish Gate bridge over the ditch on the south, the banqueting house that adorned the eastern end of her northern terrace, with steps leading down into the Little Park for her to walk in. The western end was raised so that persons in the Dean's orchard might not see into her walk. With balusters, finials, beasts along the terrace it must have been very decorative – like what one sees at Hatfield or on the honey-coloured terraces of Montacute.

The 1560's were a time of settlement, consolidation and, at Windsor, repairs – after the upheaved, sinister middle decades. On 22 April 1564 the peace treaty with France was proclaimed, 'in the Queen's Majesty's presence, going to the church; having with her Majesty the French ambassador so as nothing wanted to show contentation'. On St George's day young Charles IX was elected a member of the Order of the Garter, installed a couple of years later by proxy. It is not generally known that plans were made in 1567 for a tomb to be put up to Henry VIII; but this was not proceeded with – better not stir up that mighty dust!

After a dozen years of peace and quiet, in which Elizabeth cleverly kept her options open, a complicated crisis, both internal and foreign, crept up on her. These elements were related, and the years 1569–72 formed the watershed of her reign. Mary Stuart's disturbing presence, Norfolk's conspiracy to marry her, the rising of the Catholic Northern Earls, the Papal Bull excommunicating and deposing the Queen, the plots of the Papal agent Ridolphi with Norfolk and the aristocratic opposition leaders; the destruction of the attempts to open up trade in the Caribbean, the arrest of Spanish treasure in the Channel in reply, the Netherlands embargo on English commerce as a counter-measure: all these complexities came together.

In September 1569 when the opposition leaders, Arundel, Lumley, Pembroke, arrived at Windsor the Queen gave them a warm welcome. Cecil gave them a warmer: when they got to their lodgings they were ordered not to leave them without her permission. Meanwhile he detailed a small body of horse to shadow the movements of the shifty Norfolk, her cousin, bent on marrying Mary, in spite of Elizabeth's warning 'Look to your pillow' – in reference to what had happened to Darnley. After the collapse of Northumberland's regressive rising in the North, he was degraded from the Garter, his achievements taken down

Henry VII's Tower and Elizabeth I's gallery.

from his stall and kicked into the Castle ditch, in accordance with the regular ritual. Henry VIII had not wished to deface the register of the Order with his degradations: it was thought enough to comment on their names in the margin, 'Oh, Traitor!'

In October there arrived Alva's ambassadors from the Netherlands to discuss the detention of the Spanish treasure-ships and the stay of English shipping. They were met by Lord Hunsdon, the Queen's cousin, unbooted and refreshed in the council chamber, and then received by her and her councillors in the Presence chamber. Elizabeth put on a fine show of indignation against Alva for the arrest of shipping; she held Philip innocent. Herself, she wouldn't have dreamed of taking his money, she didn't need it; anyhow it belonged to the Genoese bankers from whom it had been borrowed, she had merely deferred its departure to verify this. The Spanish ambassador himself had requested her to take it into safe keeping from French pirates. Her show of diplomatic indignation cooling down, she said she would send commissioners to negotiate the terms of restitution of the treasure – actually she could borrow it herself and pay the interest. Thus diplomacy was conducted in the sixteenth century, though not always with such feminine virtuosity.

Excuses were made for not lodging the ambassadors in the Castle, on the ground that accommodation was too small. This was true enough. Councillors and officials had their regular lodgings – Cecil, Hunsdon, Mildmay, all had their chambers, Leicester had his study up in a tower; but there was nothing like the space available in the courts and quadrangles of Whitehall or Greenwich, Hampton Court or Richmond.

A good deal of money had been spent on necessary repairs, but now, in the 1570's, the Queen said she would have 'a gallery from her bedchamber, to go along over the Porter's lodge through the Constable's lodging, and a tennis court at the end'. The Constable was Leicester, to be followed by Lord Howard of Effingham, who became Lord Admiral in time for 1588. 'Her Highness also said that she would have a banqueting-house made ... at the east end of the terrace.' It was to be octagonal, not large, for out-of-doors collations – we should call it a summer house. Most important was the chapel – a space now engulfed in overlarge St George's Hall – with its fine woodwork, panelling, wainscoting, stalls; its four-centred ceiling with pendants and dormer windows; high up, a galleried pew for the Queen's own devotions or, more often, business. The long northern terrace remains with its stonework, though added to by Queen Victoria.

The architect for all these works was Henry Hawthorne, and his are among the earliest architectural plans to be preserved. Among the stipulations made and desires expressed to him was an amusing one from the maids of honour, who 'desire to have their chamber ceiled and the partition that is of boards there to be made higher, for that their servants look over.' Others too – and worse could happen to these frailties.

Now that there was more accommodation there were many more meetings of the Privy Council at Windsor in the later 1570's. The great hall was available for plays; we find payments to the Master of the Children of Windsor, i.e. of the Chapel, for performances, several times on St John's night. On Michaelmas day 1577 Leicester gave a feast in the hall for the French ambassador – Warwick, Húnsdon, Gresham were present to discuss the complex affairs of the Netherlands in revolt against Spain. In November Dr Dee rode over from Mortlake, and spent ten days at the Castle, to advise Walsingham and the Queen, as a geographical expert, concerning her title to Greenland, Labrador and Newfoundland. This was a consequence of Frobisher's first voyage there, upon which they thought gold had been discovered: it proved no such matter.

Among other miscellaneous activities during her periods of residence we find munitions ordered for the ten pieces of brass ordnance that garnished the castle. At the same time witches, who had made wax images of certain persons intending their destruction, were ordered to be examined by the Dean – so Deans had their uses. We regret to learn, in 1580, that Paget's son, the third Lord, 'having fallen away in religion, causing others in his country [Staffordshire] to be perverted', was committed also to the Dean for his better instruction. He was to be lodged charitably in a prebendary's house, but it seems to have done him little good. In Armada year the Dean had to examine the parson of Sonning about his popish books and 'the like trumpery' he kept. For the great excitement of that year the armour and munitions at the Castle were sent to the Tower in case of need. The danger triumphantly passed, Elizabeth's Accession Day was celebrated in 1592 with a tilt according to the ritual established by Sir Henry Lee, 'a great triumph with a course of the field and tourney'.

That summer Windsor had been visited by a German princeling, Count Mompelgart, shortly to become Duke of Württemberg, who left an unfavourable impression. For one thing, he didn't pay his bills and he seems to have taken up post-horses free of charge. For another, he had more than his share of German humourlessness; when he got back to Germany he pestered the Queen again and again for the Garter. She eventually betrayed her irritation with 'Cousin Mumpellgart', as she called him; he wrote back in typical German fashion defending himself against the calumnies and aspersions against him. He became rather too well known in England, unpopular though a figure of fun – but Elizabeth eventually yielded to his demands and nominated him in 1597. Something of all this is clearly reflected in *The Merry Wives of Windsor* of the next year, probably, 1598.

The Queen was on progress in August 1592, so she gave Mompelgart in charge of an elderly lord to amuse the German with hunting on his way through the Forest. His secretary's Journal is full of the sport they had, how 'his Highness shot off the leg of a fallow-deer,' and the dogs soon finished the animal; then his Highness shot a stag in front with an English cross-bow and the dogs worried it to death. The ceremonies and the music in St George's Chapel are more pleasing; the former being similar to the Papists (Mompelgart was a Calvinist), while the Germans were charmed by the voice of a solo-boy in the choir. The Poor Knights received attention, while the banners and shields of the Knights of the Garter inflamed him with desire to become a member. Much impressed by the wealth of the Castle, the German was inspired to leave a memento of himself by cutting his name in the lead of the highest tower. Eton had nothing whatever of interest for him.

Next year, 1593, saw a second visitation of the plague even severer than the year before – these were the years in which, owing to the closing of the theatres, Shakespeare was writing his poems and sonnets for his patron, Southampton. Elizabeth was advised to remain at Windsor until Christmas, and that autumn she occupied herself in translating Boethius' *Consolation of Philosophy*. We still have the manuscript in the hurried ageing scrawl of the eldering woman, so different from the beautiful Italian hand of her youth. She seems to have set herself a task and then raced at it. Her secretary Windebank computes the days and hours she spent upon it between 10 October and 5 November. 'Out of which twenty-five days are to be taken four Sundays, three other holidays, and six days on which your Majesty did ride abroad to take the air, and on those days did forbear to translate, amounting together to thirteen days. Thirteen being deducted from twenty-five remaineth then but twelve days. Accounting two hours only bestowed every day one with another, the computation falleth out that in twenty-four hours your Majesty began and ended your translation. At Windsor.'

Less flattering than this calculation for Majesty herself were two others that made it twenty-six and twenty-seven hours. Beginning in her own rapid cursive hand, she then got bored and dictated the prose to Windebank, while writing the verse passages herself in her idiosyncratic doggerel. One can read the impatience, and then the corrections she made. There was always plenty of other business to transact, visitors to the Court, and earlier that year masques and entertainments.

In 1598 another, more agreeable, German visited Windsor, Paul Hentzner, who gives us more interesting glimpses of the interior than Mompelgart. He mentions the room in which Henry VI was born, others containing the vast state-beds of the Tudors – of Henry VIII and Anne Boleyn, for example – all square and covered with gold and silver stuffs. There was French tapestry, curiosities like a unicorn's horn, probably a narwhal's, a cushion worked by the Queen and two bath-rooms ceiled and wainscoted with glass, which bespoke her civilised tastes.

We do not have a definite date for *The Merry Wives of Windsor*, but it is certainly between 1598 and 1601. There is no reason whatever for rejecting the old tradition that the Queen expressed a wish to see the fat knight, Falstaff, in love – a royal command to the dramatist of her Lord Chamberlain's Company. It is obvious that he put together the play in a hurry – the tradition says in a fortnight – from its ramshackle structure and its style.

It has a good deal of Windsor lore in it, and familiarity with the vicinity – probably enough, from having acted there. In the Quarto of the play – a poor reported version carried away from performance – 'Cousin Garmombles' appears. Though not named in the Folio, there is a reference to the German Duke requiring three horses of the host of the Garter Inn: 'but I'll make them pay. They have had my house a week at command; I have turned away my other guests. I'll sauce them.' There was, by the way, a Garter Inn at that time in the High Street, facing Castle Hill. As for Master Ford's distrust of his wife's virtue, Master Page 'would not ha' your distemper in this kind for the wealth of Windsor Castle.' Page again, waiting for the rest of the 'fairies' who are to mob and pinch Falstaff black and blue – as fairies did: 'we'll couch in the Castle-ditch till we see the light of our fairies.' With expectation rising in his lustful breast, Falstaff likens himself to a Windsor stag, 'and the fattest, I think, i'the Forest. Send me a cool rut-time, Jove.'

Simple, asked if he had kept a look-out for Dr Caius, replies, 'Marry, sir, the petty ward [i.e. the lower], the Park ward [the upper], every way; Old Windsor way and every way but the town way.' Mistress Page to Dr Caius: 'Master Doctor, my daughter is in green. When you see your time, take her by the hand and away with her to the Deanery, and dispatch it quickly. Go before into the Park.' Mine Host of the Garter invites Dr Caius, 'Go about the fields with me through Frogmore ... where Mistress Anne Page is at a farm-house a-feasting' (now the site of the royal gardens). Datchet Mead, where Falstaff was thrown out of the buck-basket with the dirty linen, was the low ground between Little Park and the Thames: 'among the whitsters in Datchet Mead, in the muddy ditch' – a creek existed there then near the ford. 'Mistress Ford, I have had ford enough: I was thrown into the ford.'

Then there is Herne's Oak of the last scene where Falstaff was tormented by the 'fairies'. Shakespeare loved legendary lore, and Herne the Hunter played a large part in that of the Forest and in travellers going by the old footway that went south of the Castle into its shadowy or moonlit night-terrors.

A 19th century engraving of Falstaff standing by Herne's Oak.

> Sometime a keeper here in Windsor Forest
> Doth all the winter-time, at still midnight,
> Walk round about an oak, with great ragg'd horns;
> And there he blasts the tree and takes the cattle,
> And makes milch-kine yield blood, and shakes a chain
> In a most hideous and dreadful manner . . .

Herne's Oak still stood towards the end of the eighteenth century; near it was a dell, now filled in, where the 'fairies' were to lie and pounce out on Falstaff. The play concludes, as it should, with a tribute to the Castle and its *châtelaine*:

> Elves, to Windsor chimneys shalt thou leap;
> Where fires thou find'st unraked and hearths unswept,
> There pinch the maids as blue as bilberry:
> Our radiant Queen hates sluts and sluttery . . .

(What would she think of today?)

> Search Windsor Castle, elves, within and out;
> Strew good luck, ouphs, on every sacred room,
> That it may stand till the perpetual doom
> In state as wholesome as in state 'tis fit,
> Worthy the owner, and the owner it.

There follows a garland of verse for the Garter:

> And nightly, meadow-fairies, look you sing,
> Like to the Garter's compass, in a ring:
> Th' expressure that it bears, green let it be,
> More fertile-fresh than all the field to see;
> And *Honi soit qui mal y pense* write
> In emerald tufts, flowers purple, blue, and white.

3
Stuart Crises and Amenities

THE Castle continued to be the scene of decisive events throughout the Stuart period, from James I's accession to the final decision of 1688 to settle the monarchy on a Parliamentary basis and share power between king and governing class. Actually James I and Charles I showed no particular attachment to the Castle and did nothing for it. James's interest there was in the hunting, and Charles preferred to decorate his more congenial palaces with his wonderful collections of pictures and works of art.

James's first visit to Windsor, in June and July 1603, signalised new sympathies, a change of tone and direction. True, Sir Robert Carey, a cousin of the late Queen, was made keeper of the Little Park, but he was the man who had made a getaway from her Court and ridden hard to Edinburgh to bring the news that James was at last to enter the Promised Land. Sir Henry Neville was made keeper of the game in the Forest, and he had been an Essex supporter.

The new King favoured Essex's friends, and one day something of the old enmity flared up between his right-hand man, Southampton, and Lord Grey of the opposing faction. The new Queen, in front of them all, asked tactlessly why so many great men did so little for Essex and themselves at the time of his outbreak. Southampton answered, because the Queen had been brought in as a party against them: if it had not been for that their private enemies would not have dared to oppose them. Lord Grey gave him the lie and answered that their opponents would have dealt with them well enough. Thereupon the Earl gave the Baron the lie: these fools would have fought, as they had done before, if they had not been committed to their several quarters under guard.

The next month brought down a more commanding figure. Already Lord Cobham and his brother, George Brooke, were under investigation concerning their dealings with Aremberg in the Netherlands to precipitate peace and seize the King 'and his cubs'. Ralegh was in resentful attendance upon the Court, already in marked disfavour, and was walking on a July morning upon his late Queen's terrace, waiting to hunt with the rest of the Court. Instead, out came Cecil – his former friend, whom he had been so unwise as to alienate – with a message 'as from the King', that he was to stay for examination by the Council.

He denied any knowledge of a plot to seize the King's person or of any dealings between Cobham and the Spanish envoy, Aremberg. After his examination he wrote a deposition, from which it was evident that he knew a good deal more than he had said. He was anyhow a brazen liar, as most of them knew, and from that moment – though always asserting his innocence – he could never exculpate himself. From Windsor he was on his way to the long years in the Tower, where he was more profitably employed.

With that baleful presence removed James could go on to enjoy himself after his fashion: perpetual hunting, which he relished even more than theology, the company of bishops and boy-friends, drink – it was all rather different from the domestic life of the late Queen. At Windsor there was 'some squaring between our English and Scottish lords, for lodging and other petty quarrels' – hardly room for both. Prince Henry was made a Knight of the Garter, but there was some diminution in the stately ceremonial and decorum. When Queen Anne's brother, Christian IV of Denmark, came over in 1606 for the Garter there was a scene of drunken comedy – widely broadcast at the time – in which both monarchs appeared in undignified postures.

At the Installation of 1615 there was great rivalry between the two new Knights, one English, the other Scotch, a Knollys and an Erskine, as to which would outdo the other. Knollys had the support of all his cousinage and allied families, the Scot of the Court and the new favourite, the beautiful Villiers. The sage John Chamberlain thought it were 'better forborne, but that every man abounds in his own sense'. Each peer had three hundred followers; but it was thought that the Scots were 'generally better apparelled, with many more chains of gold and better horses by means of the King's and Prince's stables'. Next year James was at the Garter Chapter: the question was whether to take away Somerset's hatchments, whose marriage with the Countess of Essex had degraded him by association with her poisoning his friend, Sir Thomas Overbury. The benevolent James, who had been so good to them, decided merely to move the hatchments higher – to make way for the new pattern of chivalry, Villiers, to become Duke of Buckingham.

In 1618 James's other interest comes into play. The best side of him was his genuine desire for peace in Europe and understanding between the Christian churches so full of hate for each other. An opportunity to advance the ecumenical cause came with the arrival in England in 1616 of a Roman prelate, Marco Antonio de Dominis, archbishop of Spalato, expedited by the wise Sir Henry Wotton, ambassador in Venice. The archbishop had become involved in the conflict between Venice and the Papacy, and when the Pope imposed a yearly pension of 500 crowns out of his archbishopric, the archbishop expressed himself horrified at the abuses of the Church, which he had not perceived before.

James, in whose breast hope sprang eternally, appointed this defecting prelate Dean of Windsor. Here for four years he made himself extremely disagreeable; though he attacked the universal claims of Rome and argued the case for national churches with much learning, he quarrelled with the canons and squeezed higher rents out of the tenants of the Chapter. He was, in fact, not only corpulent and irascible, but avaricious and dishonest. He exerted his theologian's ingenuity to find flaws in the tenants' leases so as to extract fines for his own benefit. To such an extent that, when he decided to abscond – for the climate did not agree with his health – there was found in his coffers at Gravesend some £1,700 (multiply by fifty).

He had, of course, made what he thought was his peace with the Papacy, which promised him pardon and a handsome salary on the return of the prodigal son. In return for this he declared, when he had safely left England, that he lied in every statement he had made against Rome, where only was truth and outside of which was no salvation, while the Anglican church was schismatic and degraded. It is, however, well known that no faith need be kept with heretics, and on his return to the fold he was popped into the dungeons of the Inquisition, where he shortly died. This was not enough: he was judged a heretic *post mortem* and the Holy Office, not to soil its hands, consigned the body to the secular arm to be burned along with his books.

Thus unfortunately ended this premature experiment in ecumenism.

Secular entertainments at Windsor were more agreeable. With the errant Somerset and his wife rusticated to Rotherfield Greys, the extraordinarily handsome Villiers had no rival in James's heart and was now, 1621, Marquis of Buckingham. He designed an entertainment for the King which was like no other: *The Gipsies Metamorphosed* was written by Ben Jonson, the music by Nicholas Lanier (of the family of Court-musicians, another member of which, Alfonso, was the husband of Shakespeare's Dark Lady.)★ The masque was first put on for James's reception at Burley-on-the-Hill. It met with extraordinary favour from him, since it was designed and performed by his beloved and the three good-looking young men, his brothers. James commanded it to be performed again at Windsor that September – this was the final version with Jonson's revisions and additions.

We need not go into this light-hearted masque, with its staple of gipsy-lore, telling the fortunes of the courtly auditors – the references to whom helped to make the *réclame* of the piece – the singing and dancing, the gallantry and pickpocketing (like Autolycus). Nor did the bawdy Cocklorrel song detract from its success with the taste of a time that combined the exquisite with the

★ cf. my *Shakespeare the Man.*

coarse. The four brothers were the gipsies, but the mayor and corporation of Windsor are given a hint that they are not to be taken as such and apprehended as vagrants. They proceed to 'discover' the King and to tell the fortunes of the Court from the Prince of Wales downwards. The Prince was awarded the forecast of good fortune to be expected; he was to marry the daughter of the world-empire of Spain, upon which the sun never set. (He did not; and we shall see what happened to him at Windsor.)

There follow the fortunes of the great officials, Lord Treasurer, Lord Steward, Lord Marshal, Lord Chamberlain and a couple of Scotch peers, the Marquis of Hamilton and Earl of Buccleuch. The Prelate of the Order of the Garter is saluted, and the episcopal Lord Keeper of the Great Seal, Bishop Williams, who owed his promotion to having helped Buckingham's grand marriage into the Rutland family:

> We may both carry
> The George and the Garter
> Into our own quarter . . .
> There's a purse and a seal –

the Lord Keeper's –

> I've a great mind to steal,
> That when our tricks are done
> We might seal our own pardon.

The 'Wenches of Windsor' were given a lively part along with the 'gipsies', and all their tricks were not over till 'late at night'.

We may regard the masque in its final form as a pretty addition to Windsor literature.

Next summer, while the Spanish ambassador was being entertained at the Castle, Prince Charles and Buckingham 'went every evening into the water near Eton, where the best swimming is, but so accompanied with choice company and a boat or two that there could be no danger'. Here the French ambassador took his leave, presented – according to custom – with some £2,000 for a farewell jewel. James was roving about to various parks hunting. His mania for the hunt continued to the end. At the Garter Feast of 1623 he had to be carried in a chair owing to the weakness of his legs; but his last letter to Buckingham makes an assignation to hunt with him in the Park and bring his ladies, 'Kate and Sue with their bows'.

The accession of an aesthete-king in Charles I, who prized works of art above most things, denoted new interests. The fountain in the upper yard with which

Queen Mary had finished Edward VI's conduit was taken down, to replace it with a classic structure of Hercules and Antaeus; the design was never carried out because of the onset of the King's political troubles. But he managed to present a splendid baroque service of altar-plate to St George's Chapel, executed by the finest goldsmith of the time, Christian van Vianen, whom he brought over under his patronage from the Netherlands.

James I and Prince Charles feast the Spanish Ambassadors at Windsor.

The College of canons received a distinguished recruit in the 'ever-memorable' John Hales of Eton. He was one of the finest of scholars in that scholarly time before the deluge. He wrote a tract on Schism, broad-minded and tolerant, which came to the notice of Archbishop Laud, who summoned him before him. Clarendon tells us that Laud was 'a very rigid surveyor of all things which never so little bordered upon schism' – the event of the Civil War showed how right he was. Hales found himself persuaded by the reasons urged by the Archbishop, who was a 'nimble disputant' and much more liberal intellectually than the Puritans who detested him.

In return Laud pressed upon Hales a canonry at Windsor, which he had not sought. There he made a marked figure: 'one of the least [smallest] men in the kingdom, and one of the greatest scholars in Europe.' Aubrey tells us, 'when the Court was at Windsor, the learned courtiers much delighted in his company'. His intellectual sympathies went so far as to do justice to the persecuted, but distinguished, Familists, who were undogmatic precursors of the Society of Friends. Extraordinarily for an Anglican in that time of bitter religious controversy, Hales would say that 'some time or other those fine notions would take in the world'. They have, when the absurdities of dogma have receded.

Hales was no less generous in his habits. Aubrey was told at Windsor that he was the godfather of many children, who would ask the little man's blessing as he walked to Windsor. He filled his pocket with groats for them, 'and by that time he came to Windsor bridge, he would have never a groat left.' He was, of course, thrown out of his canonry by the triumphant Puritans.

After the failure of Charles's attempt to seize the five leaders of the Parliamentary opposition to his rule, the King found it impossible to carry on government, subjected as he was to intolerable pressure at Westminster. He withdrew in dejection to Windsor, whence messages went to and fro between him and Parliament, which took the initiative and prepared to collar power. They pressed forward their bill to get control of the militia, and for taking away the bishops' votes in the Lords – wresting a solid support from the monarchy; they would conduct the war in Ireland; they proposed removing the King's appointee from the governorship of the Tower and the Earl of Northumberland from the command of the Navy for their own man, Warwick.

From Windsor Charles pitiably proposed that his proceedings against the egregious Five Members should be submitted to law. In vain: no notice was taken. The King argued that the appointment to the command of the Tower rested with him, but had to accept Parliament's; that if Northumberland was ill, Admiral Pennington was accustomed to deputise for him. An ordinance of both Houses overrode him, and he signed the Bill for taking away the bishops' votes. Very early one morning Hyde, leader of the Church party in the Commons and defender of its rights by law, came to advise the hopeless Charles, who 'knew neither how to be or how to be made great'. Shut up alone with the young lawyer – to become famous as Clarendon – a new and more cogent line became evident in the King's public statements. But it was too late: civil war was on the way, and shortly the King left Windsor, never again to see it as a free man.

Above and beyond the academic argumentation about the causes of the Civil War there remains the sheer fact of aggression in human affairs, aggressiveness as a dominant human characteristic. On the Continent the Thirty Years' War, which put Germany back for centuries – Bismarck said the scars were still visible two centuries later – was still in progress. In the 1640's France was distracted by the faction-fights of the Fronde. Even in the inert Iberian Peninsula Portugal won independence at last from Spain. Clarendon has a famous apostrophe to the happiness of England before the Civil War – if only she had known how happy she was – prosperity increasing, civilisation spreading, the nation essentially at peace for nearly forty years. Peace had indeed lasted too long: there are always fighting fools who want to fight – a recurrent feature in history – and pent-up aggressions on both sides precipitated the conflict. It proved a disaster for the country.

On 23 October 1642 Edgehill, the first battle of the Civil War, was fought. Colonel Venn was sent with twelve companies of foot to garrison the Castle and hold the approach to London. Immediately the King's magnificent service of plate was looted from St George's Chapel. Other treasures were pillaged, such as Edward IV's coat of mail with its rubies and other gems – altogether some 3580 oz. of plate were pillaged, then and later. Poor Dean Wren – Sir Christopher's father – tried to hide some of the treasures in his custody, but he succeeded only in saving a few volumes of records. The organs were broken, painted windows smashed, the town cross destroyed.

The cultivated circle around the King had done what they could to repair the artistic ravages of the Reformation. Even Archbishop Abbot, no aesthete – not even a High Churchman – had given encouragement to such glass-painters as the van Linge brothers to replace windows in the churches. Archbishop Laud also patronised the new Renaissance style with Inigo Jones's work at St Paul's; Puritans hated him almost as much for his taste as for his churchmanship: themselves preferred the rebarbative Gothic background to which they belonged.

Whatever we think of the squalor and indignity and destructiveness of the time in which we live, it is not so agonising as it must have been for a cultivated person to endure the Civil War.

In November 1642 Prince Rupert marched on Windsor; but without artillery he could not force the walls, and withdrew. Henceforth the Commonwealth had its own way there. That winter it formed the headquarters of the Parliamentarian general, Essex; five hundred deer were destroyed in the Park – there never was a proper recovery, though Charles II tried to re-stock from Germany – the park-palings were burned for firewood. Fifty-five prisoners were brought to the Castle, the canons forced out of their houses.

Though a few lived to see the Restoration, most of them died during the Interregnum, including Dean Wren, Registrar of the Order of the Garter. Our friend John Hales was reduced to straits and had to sell his fine library for a quarter of its value; with the proceeds he was able to help a colleague who, having a wife and seven children, was in extremity. Hales died in a little house next to the Christopher Inn. John Pocklington was especially unpopular with Parliament for two books he had written: one in favour of the rational enjoyment of Sunday, against their uncivilised Sabbatarianism, the other in favour of the decent treatment of the altar in church. He was immediately deprived, his books burned, and himself died, heart-broken, the same year. Thomas Soame was also obnoxious; for on the outbreak of war he 'sent all he had to the King', leaving nothing for his family of six children; himself imprisoned, they were extruded from their home. However, a favourite chaplain of the King, he was exchanged for two Puritan ministers, 'one of the best bargains his Majesty made'.

Five canons survived to be restored; Hugh Cressey, deprived, became a Benedictine and returned as chaplain to Charles II's Queen. Three of the minor canons returned at the Restoration, four had died.

The years 1645 to 1649 saw decisive events at Windsor. The New Model Army that brought final defeat to the King at Naseby received part of its training under Fairfax in the Great Park, where it was visited by its dynamic (some people thought demonic) inspirer, Oliver Cromwell. That year Colonel Venn was succeeded as governor of the Castle by Colonel Whichcote, who seems to have been a decent sort of fellow. But Parliament needed money, and in 1647 the great equestrian brass statue of St George was sold, probably for melting down; other images and materials of metal were sold, including the Renaissance candlesticks and unfinished enamels of Wolsey's tomb. That July, when the King was brought as a prisoner to the Castle for a couple of days, the bells were rung as usual on his arrival, such was the force of ancient custom.

The fact was that, though his cause had been defeated in the field, he remained the king-pin in the constitutional structure. As an old Parliamentarian peer said, 'however many times we defeat him, he remains still the king'. There followed a complex series of events, of which Windsor was the scene of some that were decisive, and in the unfolding of which the King overplayed his hand, to his own destruction.

Briefly, the game was a three-cornered one between the victorious Parliament at odds with the Army which had won the victory for it, with the King trying to bid up each side. On that brief July visit to Windsor Cromwell's able right-hand man, Ireton, put the situation in a crisp sentence to Charles: 'Sir, you have an intention to be an arbitrator between the Parliament and us; and we mean to be it between your Majesty and the Parliament.'

The Presbyterian majority in Parliament were as intolerable as they were intolerant. The terms they proposed to the King, the Newcastle Propositions, were impossible not only for him but as a basis for any government that would work; and they compounded this by antagonising the Army, holding up arrears of wages, trying to get rid of its leadership and building up a force to oppose it. Cromwell and Ireton, the ablest men on the scene, were extraordinarily patient with both Parliament and King. They tried to close with the latter, with their Heads of the Proposals, which he would have done well to accept. They went all lengths to get an agreement with him, until the Army beneath them began to be mistrustful of the negotiations and concessions to the King – as well they might, for he was not to be trusted. Like the weak man he was, he meant to cheat them. This proved fatal with such iron men.

In this dangerous situation agitation began to spread through the Army. Protests came up from the ranks against Cromwell and Ireton – moderates until the penultimate acts – 'making the King an idol, kneeling before him', kissing his hand – they were gentlemen and knew the ritual. Leveller propaganda began to spread through the Army. At Windsor in November 1647 there was an attempt at mutiny; three hundred Middlesex trained bands were sent by Parliament to make the Castle secure, but Cromwell brought mutiny to a halt with the execution of a single mutineer.

The Council of the Army transferred itself to Windsor, which was its headquarters that winter. Negotiations continued with the impossible Presbyterian leadership at Westminster, while Cromwell and Ireton worked hard to restore harmony in the Army. Charles proved equally impossible: he had sent a message to Windsor by the loyal Berkeley, who appreciated the hopelessness of it, with the virtual demand that the Army place him in a commanding position against Parliament. The Army Council met in the Town Hall while the Council of War met in the Castle.

Cromwell and Ireton treated the agitators in the Army with politic leniency and closed their ranks to form a common front against the King, up to his eyes now in negotiating with Parliament and the Scots. As part of the psycho-

Van Dyck's famous
triple portrait of
Charles I – 'a face
made for tragedy'.

logical warfare – under the name of 'exhortations to unity and affinity' to achieve a 'sweet harmony' – a ghastly three-day prayer-meeting and fast was held at Windsor, in which Cromwell, Ireton, Tichborne, Hugh Peters, officers and men alike, 'prayed very fervently and pathetically' from 9 a.m. to 7 p.m. The real business was the restoration of unity with the resolution of no further Addresses to the King. All the Council dined with the General in the Castle before their dispersal for their next moves to wrest control of the situation from Parliament.

Meanwhile Charles had come to terms with one section of the Scots to bring a Scottish army south, to start, with Royalist outbreaks in Wales, Kent and Colchester, the second Civil War. The mass of Englishmen stood aside to let their betters fight. In July 1648 there was a plan to seize Windsor Castle. In August Cromwell destroyed the Marquis of Hamilton's straggling forces at Preston. This sealed the King's fate, though he does not seem to have realised it: sunk in his dream of Divine Right and the sacrosanctity of kings, he went on spinning his webs. As Gardiner says, he never understood the gulf between himself and even the most moderate of his opponents.

The Army leaders determined to bring him to book. Charles escaped from Hampton Court to Carisbrooke Castle in the Isle of Wight; Ashburnham and Legge who had helped him to escape were sent prisoners to Windsor. The Army Council moved there, ordered the King to be held strict prisoner on 25 November, and next day engaged in another ghastly prayer-meeting, from 9 a.m. to 6 p.m., 'to direct them in the great business now in hand and that righteousness and judgment may flow in the land. It is incredible how wonderfully God appears in stirring up and uniting every man's heart as one in the prosecution of this business.' 'This business' was to bring 'the Man of Blood' to the block.

There is no doubt whatever that in so doing they believed that they were fulfilling the Lord's will. One of the regicides, faced with judgment later, said simply that they had acted 'in the fear of the Lord'. Indeed Ludlow said that they had acted in obedience to the command of Holy Writ – in which, of course, they were saturated: 'The land cannot be cleansed of the blood shed therein, but by the blood of him that shed it.'

It is faith that makes fools of humans, and it was the odious Old Testament ideology of the Puritans that ultimately ruined them. For the King's blood henceforth was to divide them for ever from the great majority of the nation; as even the Puritan historian Gardiner admits, to depose him was one thing, to kill him was quite another.

They brought him back to Windsor two days before Christmas – which they did not observe. On the way by Bagshot there was to be an attempt at escape; but the King was too heavily guarded, by ten troops of horse. Arriving in Windsor he was greeted warmly by the townsfolk: 'upon his Majesty's passing by, a great echo arose from the voice of the people crying, "God bless your Majesty" and "Send you long to reign".' If there could have been a vote of the people at large, he would have been restored. But what did that matter? As Cromwell said, who had no illusions about the people, when acclaimed by them: 'Do not trust to that: these very persons would shout as much if you and I were going to be hanged.' The King was going to be executed.

During his last three weeks at Windsor Charles remained impassive as to his fate; he seems to have had something of the sanguine optimism of his grand-mother, Mary Queen of Scots, always hoping something would turn up. He *said* that he expected to see peace in six months and himself restored, or, if not, to be righted from Ireland, Denmark or somewhere. Many people desired to see him, but were not permitted. 'His Majesty hath three new suits, two of them are of cloth with rich gold and silver lace on them, the other is of black satin, the cloak lined with plush. Since the King came to Windsor he shows little altera-tion of courage or gesture; and, as he was formerly seldom seen to be very merry or much transported with any news, either with joy or sorrow, so now – although he expects a severe change and trial – yet doth he not show any great discontent.'

He had always been an impassive man, aloof and of a royal dignity. We are reminded that when Bernini saw Van Dyck's triple rendering of his counten-ance, he said it was a face made for tragedy.

When the King left Windsor on his last journey to trial and execution out-side his palace of Whitehall, the regicide Major-General Harrison rode in the coach with him.

The body was brought back to Windsor on 7 February by the faithful Richmond, Hertford, Southampton, Lindsey and Bishop Juxon who had been with him on the scaffold at the last. That night the King's body rested in his own bed-chamber. Next day it was taken into St George's Hall. On 9 February the melancholy little procession carried the hearse across to the Chapel. The Com-monwealth Governor could not allow the Prayer Book service to be said, so the coffin was lowered in silence into the vault beside Henry VIII and Jane Seymour. As they were going to the Chapel snow began to fall, covering the coffin with a pall of white, as the faithful loved to think in after-years, 'the colour of innocency'.

As a result of the Civil War many of the finest works of architecture of the preceding century were dismantled and disappeared, not only those damaged or destroyed by war, like Basing House, Wardour and Raglan Castles, but those which went to wrack and ruin, like Henry VIII's fantastic Nonsuch, or glorious palaces like Burghley's Theobalds or Hatton's Holdenby. What losses these were!

Windsor narrowly escaped this fate, by only one vote, when several of the royal residences were sold by the Commonwealth to raise money, after the fearful waste of a superfluous war. In 1651 much of the furniture, many of the tapestries and hangings were removed; a jewel that was found, worth £6,000, was sold by order of Parliament. I do not know what happened to the royal library, but it was during this desolating period that many of the books that had been Henry's or Elizabeth's got abroad in the world.

Windsor was found a useful receptacle for prisoners in these bleak years. During the brief episode of the Second Civil War the prisoners from the Kentish rebellion were sent there; so too those that had attempted a rising in the neighbourhood of Windsor, most of them gentlemen. On the night of the King's execution the Duke of Hamilton and Lord Loughborough escaped, the former to be soon captured and executed. The Castle was crammed to capacity with Royalist officers, while barges-ful of common soldiers were sent down the river to be transported and sold into slavery in the plantations.

When things settled down temporarily under Cromwell's rule as Lord Protector, various parts of the Castle were occupied by poor persons. His government was more monarchical than the King's had been, for now the monarch was a dictator – and a very great man. Tolerant enough of religious nonsense, provided it was Protestant, he would not brook ministers meddling in politics. So in 1654 the suitably named preachers, Feak and Simpson, fetched up as prisoners in the Castle for preaching against the Protectorate.

That summer John Evelyn went to pay a pilgrimage to the Chapel, 'where they have laid our blessed martyr King Charles, in the vault just before the altar'. We see the cult of the Royal Martyr already in being, which was to exercise so powerful an influence for the rest of the century. Then the connoisseur in Evelyn takes over and he gives his opinion that 'the workmanship in stone (though Gothic) is admirable'. He thought the rooms 'of ancient magnificence', but melancholy; however, 'the terrace towards Eton with the Park, meandering Thames, sweet meadows, yield one of the most delightful prospects in the world'. A few years later, just before the return of Charles II, Mr Pepys's uncle Tom was enquiring about his chance of becoming a Poor Knight.

Twelve days after the King's happy return on Mayday 1660 the mayor and aldermen proclaimed him king in accordance with the old custom at Windsor bridge; whereupon the officers in the Castle invited them in to make sure, 'which was there also proclaimed with great joy'. The deserving poor were ejected; furniture and hangings, even the great 'unicorn's horn' preserved

St George's Chapel; an engraving by Hollar from Ashmole's *Order of the Garter* (1663).

somewhere, brought back, the Castle made ready for the return of the old ways. During the Commonwealth Charles II had held Chapters of the Garter in exile. At Canterbury on the day of his landing Monk and Montagu, prime agents in his restoration, were made Knights. For three days next year, 15–17 April, there were full feasts, ceremonies and installations, no less than twelve Knights being admitted to fill up the Order's depleted ranks. From them a large sum was raised to provide St George's Chapel with a service of plate, large gilt flagons, candlesticks, chalice – less exquisite than Charles I's; but then his son, a better politician, had less good taste. The organs were restored, the music came back; when Pepys was there in 1666 he observed great bowing to the altar. Archbishop and King had not died in vain: it was as if the Civil War had never been. (Then why have fought it?)

Above and opposite: The organ and a view of the west end; St George's Chapel from Ashmole's *Order of the Garter.*

In pursuit of present pleasure and looking upon himself 'at this time in the happiest occasion a man can be', Mr Pepys took a day off from the Navy Office in February 1666, to carry his wife down by coach to Windsor, to the Garter Inn, and there sent for a musical crony, Dr Child, who had survived the troubles. He 'carried us to St George's Chapel, and there placed us among the Knights' stalls (and pretty the observation that no man, but a woman, may sit in a Knight's place where any brass plates are set); and hither come cushions to us and a young singing boy to bring us a copy of the anthem to be sung. And here for our sakes had this anthem and the great service sung extraordinary, only to entertain us. It is a noble place indeed, and a good quire of voices.' After the service there was sight-seeing and discourse about the Order, banners and robes once more in all their glory. Mr Pepys, like Evelyn, waxed lyrical about the

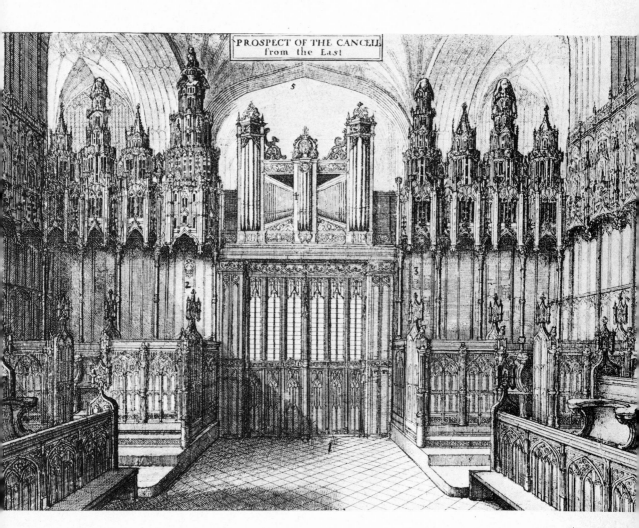

1. The West dore,
2. Body of the Church,
3. South Isle,
4. North Isle,

The Groune
George's C

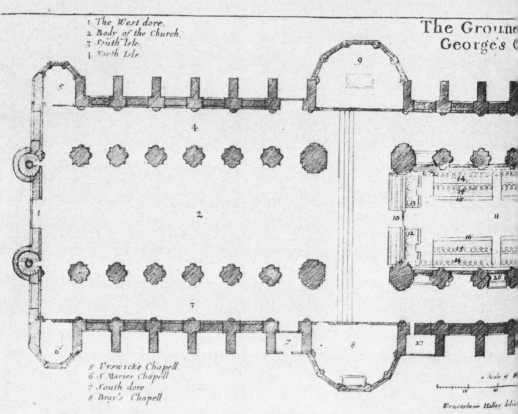

5. Vrswicke Chapell
6. S: Maries Chapell
7. South dore
8. Bray's Chapell

Wenceslaus Hollar delin

The Tombe House

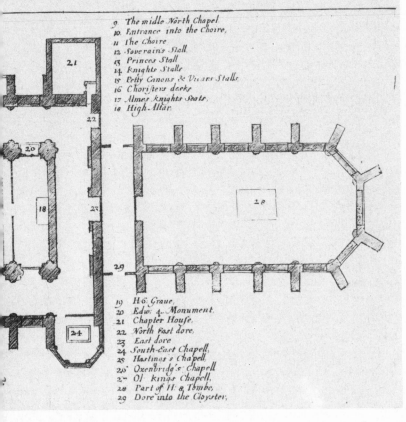

9. The midle North Chapel.
10. Entrance into the Choire.
11. The Choire.
12. Soverains Stall.
13. Princes Stall.
14. Knights Stalls.
15. Petty Canons & Vicars Stalls.
16. Choristers desks.
17. Almes Knights Seats.
18. High Altar.

19. H.6. Graue.
20. Edw: 4. Monument.
21. Chapter House.
22. North East dore.
23. East dore.
24. South-East Chapell.
25. Hastings s Chapell.
26. Oxenbridg's Chapell.
27. Ol. kings Chapell.
28. Part of H. 8. Tombe.
29. Dore into the Cloyster.

Left: South prospect and groundplan of St George's Chapel. *Overleaf:* plan of the castle exterior. From Ashmole's *Order of the Garter.*

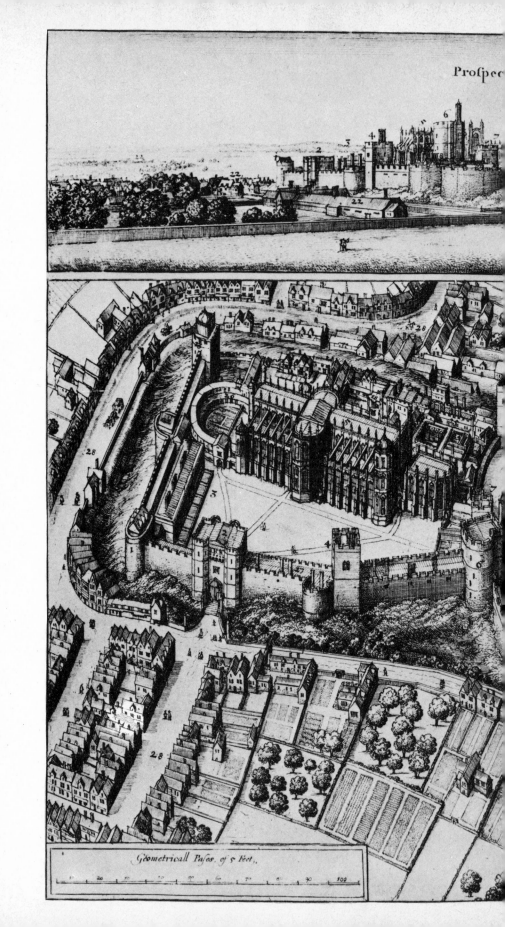

Geometricall Paſes, of 5 Feet.

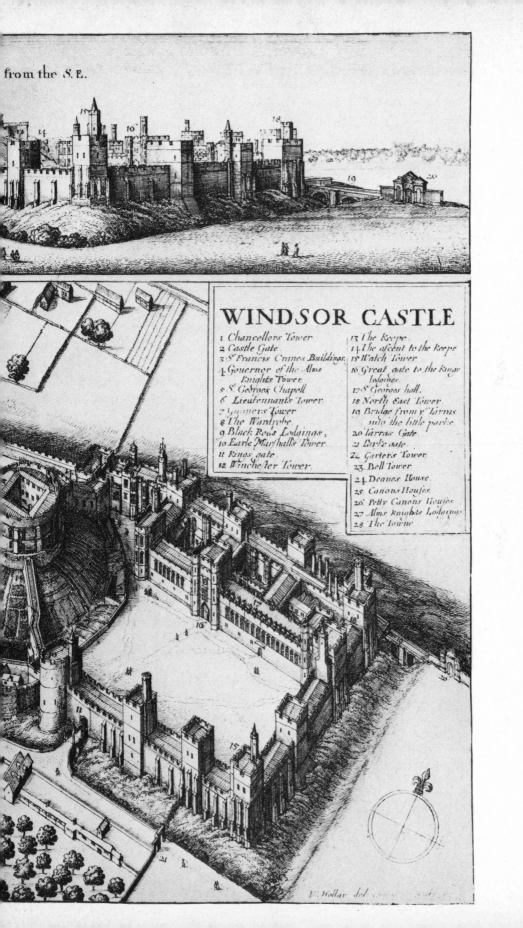

from the S.E.

WINDSOR CASTLE

1 Chancellors Tower
2 Castle Gate
3 St Francis Cranes Buildings.
4 Gouernor of the Alms Knights Tower
5 St Georges Chapell
6 Lieutennants Tower
7 Gunners Tower
8 The Wardrobe
9 Black Rods Lodgings,
10 Earle Marshalls Tower
11 Kings gate
12 Winchester Tower.
13 The Keepe
14 The ascent to the keepe
15 Watch Tower
16 Great gate to the Kings Lodgings.
17 St Georges hall.
18 North East Tower
19 Bridge from yᵉ tarras into the little parke
20 Tarras Gate
21 Parke gate
22 Garters Tower
23 Bell Tower
24 Deanes House.
25 Canons Houses.
26 Petty Canons Houses.
27 Alms Knights Lodgings.
28 The Towne

W. Hollar del.

prospect from 'the balcone in the Queen's lodgings, and the terrace and walk are strange things to consider, being the best in the world, sure'. Mrs Pepys was 'mightily pleased too, which added to my pleasure', in spite of 'giving a great deal of money to this and that man and woman'. (We learn elsewhere that the usual fee for viewing the Chapel was 2s.) Altogether, Mr Pepys sighed with contentment, 'it is the most romantique castle that is in the world'.

And a most romantic survivor from the Civil War had his residence in the Castle now – Rupert of the Rhine, Prince Rupert of so many dashing cavalry-charges on the battlefields of the late war. Made Constable of the Castle and Keeper of the Park in 1668, Rupert lived much in the Round Tower, which he repaired and made habitable. He was devoted to mechanical and scientific pursuits, in gunnery and chemistry and had his stills about the place. (A drunken orgy of Charles II's young friends one night smashed them.) Rupert had a great black dog, which accompanied him on his evening rambles about terrace and park: this made the enlightened country folk thereabouts regard him as a wizard. He had had other companionship: by a Cavalier's daughter he had a son, Dudley Rupert, whom he sent to Eton where he could watch over him.

Evelyn was struck by the contrast Rupert made in his lodgings, like the contrasting sides of his character. His hall and staircase were decorated with arms and habiliments of war, pikes, muskets, pistols, bandoliers, holsters, drums, breast- and head-pieces, arranged even as pilasters, cornices, friezes: in short, a baroque armory. When Evelyn went into the living rooms and Rupert's bed-chamber, he found them 'hung with tapestry, curious and effeminate pictures so extremely different from the other, which presented nothing but war and horror, as was very surprising and divertissant'. Evelyn was well received: supper with the Duke of Monmouth, dinner with Lord Arlington and other lords, Chapel to view the offering of the Knights according to custom, with procession and all the old ceremonies.

All was back again, once more celebrated in formal verse, this time by the laureate of the age, Dryden, in his Chaucerian romance, 'The Flower and the Leaf', with its references back to Arthur and Charlemagne's twelve knights:

> Behold an Order yet of newer date,
> Doubling their number, equal in their state:
> Our England's ornament, the Crown's defence,
> In battle brave, protectors of their prince;
> Unchanged by fortune, to their Sovereign true,
> For which their manly legs are bound in blue.
> These of the Garter called, of faith unstained,
> In fighting fields the laurel have obtained,
> And well repaid the honours which they gained.

Meanwhile the gallant Sovereign of the Order – whose companion at Windsor was not a great dog, but Lady Castlemaine – took Evelyn out into the 'balcony' over the terrace to discuss his proposed History of the Dutch War and complain of Dutch abuse of him (very understandable, in view of his collusion with Louis XIV against them). The Merry Monarch, who liked everything agreeable about him, had taken steps to abolish the irrepressible republican, Sir Henry Martyn, from his view: held prisoner, he was an 'eyesore' taking exercise upon the leads, and was rusticated to Chepstow for the rest of his life. 'The King spent most of his time in hunting the stag, and walking in the Park, which he was now also planting with walks of trees, etc.' It was at this time that the famous Long Walk, the avenue of some three miles from the nearer horizon to the Castle-walls, was planted: a happy memento of the Restoration.

A far grander monument was the entire rebuilding of the Royal Lodgings in the upper ward and along the east front, which eventuated in the finest work of secular baroque architecture in England. It is sad that almost all of it was swept away by Wyatville; only three of the rooms decorated by Verrio remain, and from those we can hardly judge for they were the least part of a grandiose achievement. By this time the palace within the Castle was not only antiquated but 'ragged and ruinous'; it was owing to the restored monarchy that it should present a more splendid image of itself, and there was the King's cousin, Louis XIV's Versailles to set a model, in the interiors, if not the exteriors. In the end, the work at Windsor had great importance and 'even greater consequences for English art. Its significance has been largely neglected, although it occupied an unparalleled position in the history of English domestic architecture, and marks the introduction of a number of new elements.' The essence of the work was the revolutionary combination, for England, of 'the three arts of architecture, painting, and carving', by which 'a true baroque fusion was achieved'.

Thus the historians of English art in the seventeenth century.

The architect who achieved it was Hugh May, overlooked in the history of our architecture, since so much of his work was destroyed; criticised subsequently too for the dullness of the exterior. In fact this was artistic decorum: he reduced his outer façades to simplicity not to challenge the medieval surroundings and subordinate his work to the concept of the castellated. But within was the colour, the sumptuousness proper to a palace. His was 'the first grand painted staircase executed in England, and its impact on the visitor emerging from the low, columned vestibule must have been tremendous'.

There were, in fact, two domed and painted staircases opening up vistas through suites of rooms as at Versailles. St George's Hall and the Chapel Royal were even more revolutionary, the latter the culminating peak of May's work and of the full baroque style in England. When one looks at his creation, walls

THE
GRAND PROCESSION
OF THE
Soveraigne
and
knights Companions
ANNO
23 CAROLI 2

Charles II in procession
to St George's Hall with
his Knights of the Garter,
a drawing by Hollar,
1672.

and ceiling all painted by Verrio, barley-sugar columns, niches and balconies beside the altar, one would think oneself in Rome. This was the trouble: the taste reflected that of a Court inclined towards absolutism, *lié* with Louis XIV, who provided it with subsidies as well as a royal mistress to keep Charles sweet; and the Catholic heir would bring it shortly to an end. It never enjoyed English sympathies.

We can trace Evelyn's response to it all, as a connoisseur, in his Diary. At the end of June 1678 he went down with the Lord Chamberlain to view the

Charles II's equestrian statue.

repairs being made 'with exceeding cost, and to see the rare work of Verrio and incomparable carving of Gibbons'. Next summer he had a hearty collation with Verrio – he had a house on the spot and was rewarded with very large sums – who 'showed us his pretty garden, choice flowers and curiosities, he himself being a skilful gardener'. Evelyn thought that Verrio's work in fresco would celebrate the King's palace 'as long as those walls last'. Alas, for such forecasts of futurity!

In July 1680 Evelyn went down, in Sir William Godolphin's coach-and-six, to see the upper ward practically completed, with Charles II's equestrian statue put up, upon Grinling Gibbons' marble pedestal with its carved relief. This was 'at the expense of Toby Rustat, a page of the backstairs, [actually, yeoman of the Robes], who by his wonderful frugality had arrived to a great estate in money and did many works of charity, as well as this of gratitude to his master, which cost him £1,000. He is a very simple, ignorant, but honest and loyal creature.' Thence on to dine at the Countess of Sunderland's and to see Signor Verrio's garden.

By the summer of 1683 the works were virtually complete. Evelyn waxed lyrical about Verrio's frescoes in St George's Hall, representing the legend of St George, the triumph of the Black Prince and his reception by Edward III. In the chapel were painted the Resurrection, the figure in the Ascension he thought comparable to the most famous Roman masters (Evelyn was too favourable). 'The Last Supper also over the altar – I liked exceedingly the contrivance of the unseen organs behind the altar – nor less the stupendous and, beyond all description, the incomparable carving of our Gibbons, who is, without controversy, the greatest master both for invention and rareness of work that the world ever had in any age.'

Evelyn's unmeasured enthusiasm tells us what contemporary connoisseurs thought of Charles II's work at Windsor, whereas from the history text-books one would never learn that he built anything. The surroundings of the Castle were tidied up and much improved too. The terraces were brought almost round the castle; 'the grafts [ditches] made clean, even, and curiously turfed; also the avenues to the new Park and other walks planted with elms and limes, and a pretty canal and receptacle for fowl. Nor less observable and famous is the exalting of so huge a quantity of excellent water to the enormous height of the Castle, for the use of the whole house, by an extraordinary invention and force of Sir Samuel Morland.'

After the destructiveness of the Civil War the Restoration was a wonderful period for repairing, rebuilding, planting and improving all over England. Many of the works of that more hopeful time have come to an end in ours; Hugh May's Windsor disappeared under the heavy hand of Wyatville, but at least he left us as much that is worthy of respect and even admiration. One work was planned which, we may regret, did not come into being. Before the idiocy of the Popish Plot engulfed the country, the House of Commons made a large grant for a monument to Charles I, and Sir Christopher Wren designed an exquisite mausoleum, like a little dome of St Paul's. There was to be a chaste rusticated base, then a drum with coupled columns and a dome with lantern, Fame blowing her trumpet at the summit. Grinling Gibbons prepared designs, one of them for a statue in bronze, standing on a plinth supported by the heroic virtues, with the vices of Rebellion, Heresy, Hypocrisy, and Envy being squashed beneath. Though the vices were appropriate enough to the case, the heroic may be thought to have been somewhat wanting in Charles I.

Anyhow the troubles unleashed by the Popish Plot frustrated the intention. The building was to have gone up on the site of the Albert Memorial Chapel. The Castle lost what would have been a distinguished work of baroque art; perhaps the Gothic chapel is more appropriate as it is.

Such was the background to the business and frolics, the jollities and junketings, the politics and intrigues, of Charles II's Court. He loved being at Windsor, it was really his favourite residence; he usually contrived to spend the late summer there and sometimes other parts of the year – September best of all for the hunting. Sir Robert Southwell pined, from foetid Whitehall: 'Windsor is a charming place'; everybody felt better for the air there. In July 1678, in the middle of the troubles of the Popish Plot, 'his Majesty is grown impatient to be at Windsor'. In April next year the King had 'an inclination to see Windsor'; in June, the refrain is 'his Majesty hopes soon to be at liberty to go to Windsor'.

There were all sorts of entertainments, good, bad and doubtful. Charles enjoyed not only hunting, but the fishing at Datchet – where Falstaff was tumbled in – hawking along the river-banks, open and unobstructed then, horse-racing on the Flats, tennis in the new court he made, and cock-fighting all the menfolk enjoyed. Charles even liked walking, and took long walks in the Park. Then there were the ladies: he built a house outside the walls for Nell Gwyn, which was to have a more respectable future; the Duchess of Portsmouth (the 'French whore' of the story, as opposed to 'the English' one) having her lodgings within the Castle. Charles tried to make up by a good deal of exercise by day for the ravages to his constitution incurred at night; he was only fifty-five, however, when he died.

In August 1674 there was an elaborate mock-siege of Maestricht set up in a meadow below the Terrace, which was witnessed by a thousand spectators, Evelyn and Pepys among them – who returned to London together, arriving at 3 a.m. Charles's beloved bastard, Monmouth, had fought gallantly at the real

Sir Christopher
Wren's proposed
mausoleum for
Charles I, 'like a
little dome of St
Paul's'.

siege of Maestricht the year before. Now it was reconstructed, the town
attacked by Monmouth and his uncle the Duke of York – against whom as king
the nephew was to rebel and by whom be executed: that was the real thing,
only eleven years away. Now there were trenches opened, raised batteries,
counterscarps, 'great guns fired on both sides, grenados shot, mines sprung, and
– what is most strange – all without disorder, or ill accident ... and was really
very divertissant.' Anyhow, a better way of letting off men's aggressions than a
civil war.

'His Majesty being so much at Windsor', as Sir Leoline Jenkins of All Souls and
Secretary of State wrote, entertainments and politics are reflected in all their
variety in the state papers. The House of Commons expressed its anger at the
members of the Cabal ministry by taking up a trivial incident at Windsor,
when one of them, Buckingham, as Master of the Horse, tried to force the

Racing at Datchet: Charles II in the Royal stand and the castle in the background.

King to stay longer at a drinking bout than he wished, taking hold of his bridle. Sir Winston Churchill in the Commons came to the defence of the indefensible Duke. At a Garter Installation the rivalry between Denmark and Sweden was reflected in the Danish envoy objecting to his master's stall being placed below the King of Sweden's, though the Danish king had been installed while still a prince. He claimed precedence for the older kingdom: not allowed.

In August 1675 we find a typical note from the King: 'My Lord Keeper, I desire that you would dispatch the patent for the Duke of Richmond as soon as may be. I am your affectionate friend, C.R.' This referred to his bastard son by the French Duchess of Portsmouth, then a child of three; Louis XIV, whose agent she was, added the dukedom of Aubigny for good measure. It was all very unlike the domestic life of Oliver Cromwell. The problem was what to call these royal brats, there were so many of them. Another personal note reads: 'Upon better thoughts I do intend that the Duke of Richmond's name shall be Lennox, therefore the warrant and the bill must be changed. C.R.' In any case, even the loyal Clarendon thought the King displayed too much familiarity, unlike the natural dignity of his father at the worst of times. People took advantage of the son's too easy good nature. One night in February 1677 a manservant of his witty crony, Tom Killigrew, was killed or killed himself in the very next chamber to the king. Charles at once left for London. Next year four ruffians – three of them Irish – were sent down to kill him, but were apprehended in time.

Queen Catherine, who was portrayed, poor lady, as the Virgin in one of Verrio's ceilings, took her place in the variegated female entourage. For her journey down in the summer of 1678 two new extraordinary wagons were needed for the service of Coffers, two for the Bedchamber and its ladies, one ordinary one for Sir John Arundell, a Household official and a good Catholic, and one for the Queen's Chapel – that would be her priests, including her confessor she could hardly be without.

These were the years of the Popish Plot, 1678, 1679, 1680, when London and Westminster were in the grip of anti-Catholic mob-hysteria, worked up by the infamous Titus Oates and exploited for party purposes by the Whigs under the brilliant malevolence of Shaftesbury. He had been a member of the Cabal, then turned his coat. There is a resigned sort of dignity, in all the high fever of politics, in Charles's note from Windsor in the summer of 1678 approving the exclusion of two leading JPs in Norfolk: 'there is no objection against it but in disobliging those sort of people who will never be obliged, and any countenance I give them is only used against myself and government. C.R.' One hears the accents of his polite but weary cynical voice.

Next August 1679 the reptilian Shaftesbury, expected at Windsor, was 'to be plainly admonished that it was better to have him a declared enemy out of his post than in it'. That week Charles fell dangerously ill – the political hysteria still at its height. It may have been a foretaste of the stroke that killed him; the doctors thought it was 'occasioned by staying too late in the evening a-hawking, after having played at tennis in the morning'. He was let blood, made to rest, and sweated; and the fever subsided. The Popish Plot agitation continued all the time, and the obstinate James, who had contributed so largely to it by his conversion and had had to be sent into exile, returned and went down to Windsor in case of his brother's death. 'Both City and country were sensible how much depended on his well-being', and from that fright dated the reaction in his favour. His recovery was attributed to 'that extraordinary calm temper that he has showed in all his sickness . . . he never changed from that calmness that he had in health.' He certainly needed it, when people were so mad. Soon he was 'sitting up in bed, eating mutton and partridges and discussing the forthcoming visit to Newmarket'. The Whig leaders went on with their venomous campaign.

Nell Gwyn and others had had a fright too, and wondered what would become of them. An official wrote to the Duke of Ormonde, Lord Steward of the Household, 'Mrs Nelly had commanded me to present her faithful service to your Grace, and is assured, she says, of your kindness'. It appears that the Exchequer had taken the opportunity to put a stop to her pension (for services rendered). 'She presents you with her real acknowledgments for all your favours, and protests she would write in her own hand, but her wild characters, she says, would distract you.' It appears that the former orange-girl was illiterate, but her son was made Duke of St Albans, and his too-generous father was anxious to find some lands to settle on him.

When Charles, with his inexhaustible vitality, was out and about again he was to be seen measuring the flow of water under Sir Samuel Morland's pump by his minute watch. Like his cousin Rupert, Charles ii was much interested in scientific experiments and was very pleased with Morland. As well he might be, for after various improvements the engine filled up a great cistern which supplied water direct to the Royal Apartments – and Sir Samuel received his ribbon and medal. In September Monmouth – who had, like James, been sent off into exile to calm things down – returned without permission to see his father at Windsor. He was tenderly received, but had to be sent off again at once until the political fever roused by the Popish Plot subsided.

But all the Catholicism about in the Court, and the proselytising, had a very bad effect in a country that was madly Protestant. Young Sir William Clifton was proposing to marry a Papist, by which he would 'infallibly lose both his interest and friends in these parts', (Nottinghamshire). Lord Chancellor

Finch specially went down to Windsor, where Clifton 'was become very familiar and conversant in Court'. The young man kept away; *how* he got to Windsor and 'by whose conduct God knows, but there the business began'.

Others besides God knew how another young spark, Lord Courcy, heir to a great peerage, got to Windsor and exposed himself to other dangers. A Mrs Wall at Oxford, with whom he was having an intrigue, put him up to it, 'he being quite sick of Oxford'. She instigated his coming to Windsor, though under age, 'to enter into fortune and preferments and to shake off all other pedantical ways'. He told Sir Robert Southwell, Clerk of the Council, that his tutor's uncle, a bishop, had given him leave. Southwell put him off by saying that 'he ought not to be seen at the Court until his final orders came. But his Lordship – to be true, I suppose, to the assignation long before made – passed over the usual forms and *said* he had leave.' Sir Robert expressed himself doubtful of the young man's 'future course', but it must be said that the greatest grandees set him no better example.

Having surmounted the agitations of the Popish Plot – though Charles was 'really incensed' with the machinations of the Jesuit Coleman, which had given Titus Oates his cue and his original excuse – and saved his throne for his Catholic successor, Charles's last years were quieter and he enjoyed a measure of independence, through the enormous subsidies he extracted from cousin Louis. (This enabled him, among other things, to build a Wren palace at Winchester, nearly finished when he died.)

In June 1682 when Charles caught chill again at Windsor James came south from Scotland, where he was governing, to visit him. Lord Sunderland, another twister, was back at Court, all bypast faults forgiven, at the intercession of the Duchess of Portsmouth (there was no Duke). That was another little thing those ladies were for – acts of mercy and kindness mingled with politics. Sunderland had been with the Whigs and in correspondence with their residual legatee, William of Orange; but now at the end of July he was taken down to the Castle in the Duchess's coach and received in her lodgings by the King. Sunderland gave assurances of good behaviour for the future. 'Many honest men are alarmed at it, but not I', said James – stupid as usual, for he ultimately had most cause to be. Sunderland encouraged him as king along the path he wanted to go, to his own perdition – though not, of course, that of his precious soul.

James was meaner, and financially more careful, than Charles, who was at Windsor in April and May 1683, being teased by Scotch affairs and Scotch lords badgering him. James went into the King's Scottish revenues, and found that he had been scandalously overcharged and rooked. 'I have been attacked by several ladies already, as well as by others, and shall still do my part, that his Majesty's charge may not be increased.'

Sir Samuel Morland, the inventor whose new pump
brought water up to the Castle.

In 1683 James found a suitable Catholic husband, Sir Henry Waldegrave, for his daughter by Arabella Churchill. It would seem that the marriage, in the circumstances, took place in July. For on the last of the month Charles and his Queen went to Windsor; James and his wife, with the new married couple were to follow next day, 'whence I shall have more leisure to answer' about Scotch affairs under discussion. Charles had been accustomed to confront his troubles with good humour and discuss affairs with some levity. When the Commissioners of the Admiralty were summoned to Windsor in Maytime 1682, after dinner they asked his Majesty for his commands. He said blithely that the Council was to meet at 4 p.m., meanwhile 'he had nothing for us but positive divinity'. However, matters had been discussed in his bed-chamber the night before, and on the matter of passports and fees to the Secretary of State the 'King was well prepared', no doubt by the Secretary of State, who was to have £500 a year and 20s for each passport. Thence flowed the stream of funds that watered Secretary Coventry's glades at charming Minster Lovell and enabled him to entertain his friends freely in his retirement.

In Charles's last year James was at his ear with advice, as his inevitable successor. In the summer of 1684 he was writing from Windsor protesting that the 'kind usage Monmouth has from the Prince of Orange scandalises all honest people here and encourages the factious party'. Charles had always had a tenderness for his eldest bastard, who was as irresponsible as he was handsome. In spite of being as handsomely provided for with a pension of £6,000 a year and a marriage to the richest heiress in Scotland – whom he neglected for a more appetising morsel – he had lent himself to the Whig caucus in the hope of making himself king. When his father died, however, he was succeeded by James, for whose rightful succession Charles had so patiently, skilfully, and in the end successfully fought.

Right: Edward IV, a window in St. George's Chapel.
Overleaf: Windsor Castle and Mound from a map of 1607.

4
The Revolution and Queen Anne

WHEN one looks at Kip's views of the Castle, in his *Britannia Illustrata* of 1709, one sees how it emerged from Charles II's ministrations and remained essentially unaltered for the next century. There is Hugh May's palace with tall classical round-headed windows along the *piano nobile*, entrance-gate slightly to one side of the long regular front. The east front was also regularised, but with its four castellated towers retained. A new raised terrace went right round east and south fronts, ditch outside, to the medieval walls encircling the Round Tower. Extensive formal gardens occupied the southern slopes down to and beyond Nell Gwyn's house, inherited by her son the Duke of St Albans, subsequently bought by chaste George III for his (legitimate) daughters, and later the home of the *married* quarters of the Guard.

Here was the background to the historic decisions of 1688, the last until we come to the abdication of Edward VIII, if that is worthy of being regarded as one.

Charles II's efforts had procured a peaceful and even friendly accession for James II. The Whiggish Sir William Temple, who had nevertheless been a good servant of the state under Charles II, on his way to his new home at Moor Park turned aside to pay homage to the new king at Windsor. James reproached him for not entering his service and insisting on retirement; Temple promised to live always as 'a good subject'. He regarded this as a pledge; though a friend of William III, who several times sought his advice, he would not go back on his word.

As with the Pilgrimage of Grace in 1536 and Wyatt's rebellion against Mary, so Monmouth's rebellion against James II in the summer of 1685 merely strengthened the monarch's hand and encouraged him to go further along his chosen road than was good for him. James came into the open with his Catholicism and showed his determination to advance his Church all he could – very unwise in one who owed his succession to the Church of England and his seat on the throne to its support. People were prepared to put up with him, in the expectation that his Protestant daughter Mary and her husband, William of Orange, would succeed after him.

Above left: A watercolour by Hollar, c. 1659, probably painted when he was at Windsor with Ashmole.
Below left: The north terrace at sunset, c. 1790, painting by Paul Sandby.

The view from the north – J. Kip, *Britannia Illustrata* 1709.

The loyal Evelyn, who had already been scandalised by the ostentation and ceremony surrounding the King's public attendance at Mass at Whitehall, was the reluctant witness of similar misbehaviour on the part of the official head of the Church of England, at Windsor in September 1685. He had been to matins and communion 'in the cathedral' – as St George's was commonly called for the next century. 'Then I went to hear a Frenchman, who preached before the King and Queen in that splendid chapel next St George's Hall. Their Majesties going to Mass, I withdrew.' Instead he went to contemplate Verrio's frescoes in the hall, now complete, which 'I think equal to any, and in many circumstances exceeding any, I have seen abroad.' Evelyn had been abroad, but I think we must put this judgment down to his patriotism.

Evelyn went to dinner with a large company at Lord Sunderland's, now Secretary of State and determined to worm his way into being principal minister to the monarch stupid enough to declare, 'having already risked the loss of three kingdoms by declaring himself a Roman Catholic, he would not belie his own past: he was resolved to use the powers placed in his hands by Almighty God for the re-establishment of the true religion'. This reliance upon the Almighty to advance one's own prejudices was apt to prove a bruised reed, as Mary Tudor had found. The conversation at Windsor that day was all about who would succeed the Lord Chancellor, fallen dead. Everybody guessed it would be the horrid Judge Jeffreys who was making history by his savage sentences upon Monmouth's deluded supporters in the West Country. It proved to be so; the *mise-en-scène* for the Revolution against the fatuity of James was taking shape before men's eyes. One could have foretold what would happen; indeed clever Charles II had already done so: he gave his brother three years. It proved precise.

We can watch James at his nonsense at Windsor through the medium of the state papers. There was a move to replace the upright Clarendon as Lord Lieutenant of Ireland, by the irresponsible and light-weight, but Catholic, Dick Tyrconnel who had been in a plot to murder Cromwell, and was one of the 'men of honour' who combined to dishonour Clarendon's sister, James's first wife. We see very well what Sunderland – who had no beliefs, but was on his way to becoming a convert to Catholicism, with the best of intentions – thought of James when he said 'there was no leading the King but by a woman, a priest, or both'. He fixed Tyrconnel's appointment, which had the inevitable consequence of upsetting the settlement of Ireland. They then got rid of Catherine Sedley, James's mistress, an intelligent woman who had been a sensible influence. This pleased the Queen, Mary Beatrice of Modena; Sunderland converted himself and became James's chief adviser, except for the Jesuit Petre, promoted to the Privy Council. All was set for an ultramontane course.

As a Divine Right monarch James touched for the King's Evil, as that religious person, his brother, had done before him. But, as a true believer, the King now dropped the Dean of the Chapel and his Windsor chaplains from attending the services, substituting the Latin use and his own priests. No doubt he thought it more efficacious. The disused chapel Cardinal Wolsey had intended for himself was fitted up for Roman services, and in the secret service accounts – though the services were public enough – we find large payments to a French interior decorator for vestments, linen, candlesticks, etc.

In July next year there took place a demonstration such as had not been seen in England since the unfortunate reception of Cardinal Pole, which brought no benefits to the rule of Mary. This was the reception of a Papal Nuncio, Monsignor Dadda, domestic prelate to the Pope. The government had the sense to see that this would never do in Protestant London, where it would have raised a riot, but at Windsor it provided at least a spectacle and drew crowds. Altogether there were some thirty-six coaches-and-six, the Duke of Grafton, another of Charles II's bastards, in the King's coach, with the prelate in purple, gold crucifix on breast. Two sycophantic Anglican bishops, Durham and Chester, sent their coaches though they knew better than to be there. The Duke of Somerset refused to conduct the Papal emissary, as contrary to the laws: he was dismissed from his post in the bedchamber, his place being taken by a backwoods Scotch peer, a Papist.

James went forward like a somnambulist to the precipice not far off. The day after the reception he promoted the Catholic Strickland to the command of the Navy, hoping for his support when needed; later this had to be rescinded for the Protestant Dartmouth, in attendance that day. James took the Church of England at its word; for decades now it had been preaching Passive Obedience to the monarch. But, in politics, no-one holds to his word contrary to his interests; James tried the Church of England too hard, and it went back on him. With the unexpected birth of a Catholic son and heir – whom Protestants affected to believe supposititious – the invitation went over to William to intervene in England.

In the rapid series of events in which William took over power his four days at Windsor were decisive. On learning that James had fled the country William at once moved up towards the capital, reaching the Castle on 14 December. Next morning he was mortified by the news that James's flight had been stopped by some fishermen at Faversham. William at once sent off Zuylestein with the message that James remain at Rochester for the present; but he was already on his way back to Whitehall. Here was a dangerous *impasse*: with the sentimental English sympathy was already rising for a fallen monarch. 'Compassion has begun to work', wrote Burnet, a Scot and no sentimentalist.

James sent the Huguenot general, Feversham, proposing terms of accommodation. William at once consigned him to the Round Tower. By now many of the peers had converged on Windsor, particularly the powerful leaders of the Northern wing in the combination against James's rule. The Prince sent a deputation of them ordering his father-in-law to remove from Whitehall to Ham House. This propulsion completed James's disarray, and he renewed his intention of flight, when no impediment was placed this time in his way. On 16 December William found time to write to Dartmouth in command of the Navy, which had come over to William, commending him for standing firm 'to the Protestant religion and liberties of England, to which not only the Fleet but the Army and the nation in general have so frankly concurred'. Louis XIV had offered James an army to hold Portsmouth and keep open communications with France. Burnet says, 'all the priests were for this, so were most of the Popish lords'. James's soldierly young son by Arabella Churchill, Berwick, was

Left: 'Dutch William, a truly great man, never popular in England' in his Garter robes.
Above: Windsor Castle, c. 1700, in the reign of William III.

in command, but had to surrender it. Before leaving Windsor for Whitehall, William sent his orders taking over the garrison and command at Portsmouth. James's fantasy-world collapsed like a house of cards.

Dutch William, a truly great man – and never popular in England – was left to pick up the threads of government in inconceivably difficult circumstances: a European war on his hands, the organisation of Europe's resistance to the overweening ascendancy of Louis XIV – in which William, not James, had the support of the Pope – the kingdoms divided, with Ireland, of course, supporting James. William did not much care for Burnet, but he rewarded his services with the bishopric of Salisbury and, with Windsor in his diocese, he was sworn Chancellor of the Garter. Burnet remained there through the anxious summer of 1689 which saw William's victory at the Boyne and the naval defeat off Beachy Head. Once a week he went up to wait on Queen Mary at Whitehall deputising manfully for her husband. The new bishop divided his year: eight months at Salisbury, four months at Windsor. Eight years later, when appointed tutor to Anne's son Prince William, Burnet was summoned to Windsor, where he begged to resign his diocese. King William refused and suggested a compromise: in winter Burnet would live at St James's, in summer with the Prince at the Castle, leaving ten weeks a year for visiting his diocese. The good bishop gave the whole of his salary, £1,500 a year, to charitable uses.

Meanwhile a voice from the past was heard. Charles II's widow, Catherine of Braganza, apprehensive of disturbance in London – where the Catholic chapels had been wrecked and fired by the mob – expressed herself willing to go to Windsor, 'to avoid all occasions of jealousy or dissatisfaction to the government'. Sensible woman – her future was provided for by her return to Portugal, where she made a respected and successful Regent. In June 1692 Evelyn was taking his grandson, aged ten, to Eton; he took the opportunity to look in at the Castle, where he found all well 'and very neatly kept as formerly, only the arms in the guard-chambers and Keep were removed and carried away'. A Revolution had passed over, leaving it unscathed.

William III was so much abroad fighting his wars, and had to be in Holland part of each year as Stadtholder, that he had not much time for Windsor in the early years of his reign. But he never overlooked it – everything was present to that able, planning, overburdened mind. Even in the crisis of December 1688 he found time to order 108 red deer from Germany for Windsor Forest. The red deer-walks extended as far as Bagshot, Sandhurst, Easthampstead. In time for next St George's day, 1689, he sent his mandate for replacing James II's banners from the Chapel by his own and setting up the new Knights', Marshal Schomberg and the Earl of Devonshire, among his leading supporters. Another

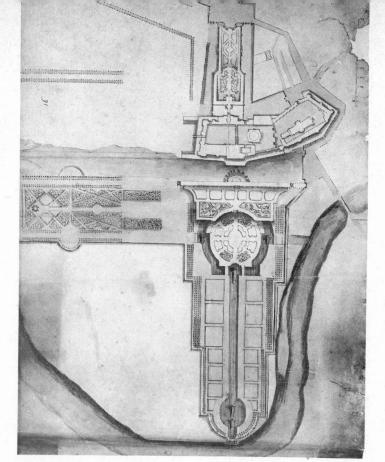

Right & below:
Christopher Wren's
plans for improving
the castle commis-
sioned by William III
in 1692.

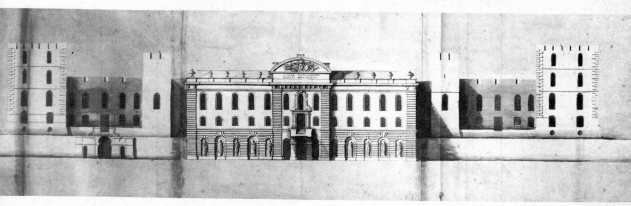

staunch supporter was the Protestant Duke of Norfolk – of that family by no means so consistently Catholic as is popularly supposed: as Constable he made a careful custodian of the Castle in William's absence. In 1692 William ordered Sir Christopher Wren to make a survey of the Castle environment and had it in mind to complete his uncle, Charles II's work, with a great classic building on the south side of the upper ward to balance Hugh May's on the north side.

121

View from the south with the Duke of St Alban's house in the left
foreground. From J. Kip, *Britannia Illustrata* 1709.

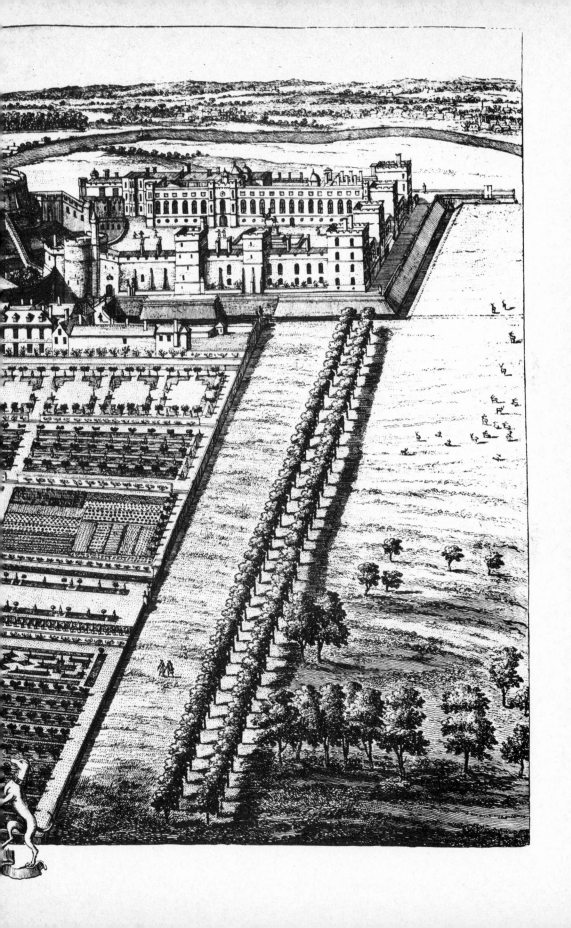

Queen Anne, with her son William.

The whole thing was to be regularised, with a gate in the middle where George IV's Gate now is. But William was too heavily engaged with building Kensington and the splendid work he got Wren to do at Hampton Court, and these were the places where he mostly resided.

Princess Anne could not bear her brusque and dominating brother-in-law, who was much more master in his kingdom than ever her father had been, and she was jealous of her popular sister, Queen Mary. (In her private correspondence with the Marlboroughs William was always 'Caliban'.) But, after the Queen's death, there had to be a reconciliation and Anne, who always loved Windsor, came down a great deal with her husband, Prince George of Denmark, and their little boy William, the presumptive heir. The taciturn King, who had no children of his own, was fond of the child and had him installed as Knight of the Garter, with more than accustomed splendour in 1696, though the boy was only seven and far from strong. William himself came down every year to observe the anniversary of Queen Mary's death, very strictly, fasting all day, shutting himself up so that no-one was admitted but his attendants.

After the Peace of Ryswick in 1697 William came down regularly. That year there were large payments for furnishing his bedchamber and private drawing room. In January 1698 the Czar Peter spent some days at the Castle in the care of Lord Romney, William's handsome young Sidney favourite. Another earlier favourite was Bentinck, promoted Earl of Portland, who reported from Paris: 'M. Le Notre [who designed the gardens at Versailles] will make me a plan for the gardens contemplated at Windsor.' William enjoyed the hunting and shooting there: 'the open weather kept him longer abroad than he intended.' This spring he had public receptions of ambassadors, French and Swedish, for the latter sending his coaches as far as Slough to meet him. In the Forest there was stag-hunting and coursing the hare; but there was a late fall of snow, and the cold brought the King back to Kensington – he was asthmatic, a great spirit in a frail frame – before leaving for Holland.

Meanwhile we find Matthew Prior, on embassy in Paris, writing to Keppel, (another favourite, made Earl of Albermarle), describing in French how they had all observed St George's day with red crosses in their hats; when he drank the Sovereign's health that night, he would add Albemarle's in the hope of seeing him soon installed. In July the Duke of Newcastle – another Revolution magnate – gave a fabulous feast at his installation. Later that year the King came down according to custom to observe Queen Mary's death. He expressed himself satisfied with what was being done in the Park. But, 'as it is one of the finest summer seats, so it is the worst in winter . . . his Majesty found the air too sharp to continue there.'

Princess Anne and Prince George had their own house at Windsor, and one finds them there now every summer – in 1698 she describes herself 'a perfect cripple' with the gout. In July 1700 her son fell dangerously ill 'of a malignant fever'. An express went off to the King in Holland. Within a few days the boy was dead: 'the affliction their Royal Highnesses are in is not to be expressed, and so is the whole Court'. With him their hopes of a family were extinguished, and an Act of Settlement was necessary assuring the succession to the Protestant, i.e. Hanoverian, line.

At the end of August a cleric reports that Prince George 'now goes a-hunting, shooting and the like. And I hope in a little time the Princess will use those diversions she used to do, and her sorrow will abate in time, which as yet she cannot wholly overcome.' Nor did she overcome her resentment against Mr Caliban – she inherited her father's resentful temper. Portland had been made keeper of the game, and when he sent to know how many bucks he should kill for her use, she angrily replied she would order as many as she had a mind to herself.

She shut herself up in her close association with the Marlboroughs. She had written to Sarah that Sir Benjamin Bathurst had the disposal of the office of page of presence, and 'I am fearful he should think I am like the rest of the world, desirous to get all I can for my own interest.' As if anyone could think such a thing of these people! Here is Marlborough reminding Sir Benjamin of 'the diamonds I spoke to you of at Windsor, for buckles and tags – when it comes in your way and you have leisure; I am not in haste for that matter'. Marlborough's well-known courtesy never got in the way of what he wanted; it was rather an instrument used for getting it.

In 1701 Anne is at Windsor again complaining at the 'ill-natured, cruel proceedings of Mr Caliban, which vexes me more than you can imagine: I am out of all patience when I think I must do so monstrous a thing as not to put my lodgings in mourning for my father'. This was politics, of course: it was impossible to allow a public demonstration of grief for James II. Anyhow, Princess Anne had been as much involved in getting rid of him as anybody else, and was shortly to profit greatly from it. When she became Queen, her friend Sarah said she never heard her express a word of regret for him. At the moment she was more interested in seeing a copy of his will, which she asked the ambassador in Paris to send over.

Next year Mr Caliban himself was dead; and Queen Anne and the Marlboroughs were in clover.

Anne had been fond of Windsor since she was a girl. At fifteen she was writing thence to Lady Apsley – in the affected style they all caught from reading the sentimental romances of Mademoiselle Scudéry and such: 'I hope you will not deny me this request, that if you won't let my fair Semandra come to tarry, you would let her come to go back at night. I had rather you would let her come to stay ...' This was Lady Apsley's daughter: perhaps she feared for her virtue at Charles II's Court. Anne's next letter is to the fair Semandra herself: 'I do assure you I do love you dearly, and not with that kind of love that I love all others who proffer themselves to be my friends ... Pray, therefore, dear Semandra, love me as well as ever ... and forgive and believe your Ziphares.'

There was a hot-house atmosphere in these female affections around Mary and Anne, which broke out into ulcerated jealousies later over Sarah Marlborough and her poor relation, Abigail Hill, who supplanted her in Anne's heart. That was in the sad future. With the fair Semandra safely married to Sir Benjamin Bathurst, Comptroller of Anne's Household, Ziphares could assure her that 'though he [sic] changes his condition, yet nothing shall ever alter him from being the same to his dear Semandra that he ever was.' Then, reverting to her normal sex, Anne bids Lady Bathurst send her tailor down to Windsor: 'I want him mightily to mend one of my gowns, and bid him bring me a pair of bodys [bodices] to wear with a manto.'

The great emotional affair of Anne's life was her love for Sarah Churchill, who was singularly unresponsive, for she was in love with her husband. Once, when they were riding by Windsor Lodge, Sarah wished that she lived there for the air. The moment Anne became Queen, she wrote, with her usual oblique delicacy, asking if Sarah would accept it for life. 'Anything that is of so much satisfaction as this poor place seems to be to you, I would give Mrs Freeman [i.e. Duchess Sarah] for all her days.' As things turned out, it was lucky for Sarah that the grant was for life – it long survived their friendship, Anne's life and George I's, and well into that of George II.

The Marlboroughs lived there a great deal – the Duke died there in 1722. Sarah wrote that it was 'of all the places that ever I was in the most agreeable'. In 1708 Anne had made her Ranger of Windsor Great Park. In later years, one of her *protégé* Walpole's misdeeds was that he withdrew her £500 a year as Ranger – the state had already made her virtually a millionairess – and, still more annoying, he refused to bar Nell Gwyn's son, the Duke of St Albans, from driving through the Park to bait her. Nevertheless, 'as I have altered Windsor Lodge, 'tis a thousand times more agreeable than Blenheim, and I shall pass the greatest part of my life there ... In a lodge I have everything convenient and without trouble.' She had had enough of palaces, and couldn't bear Blenheim.

Since the Queen was so much at Windsor – either in her little house in the Little Park or at the Castle for Courts and formal occasions – many of her

Plan of Windsor Castle, 1738, dedicated to Charles, third Duke of Marlborough.

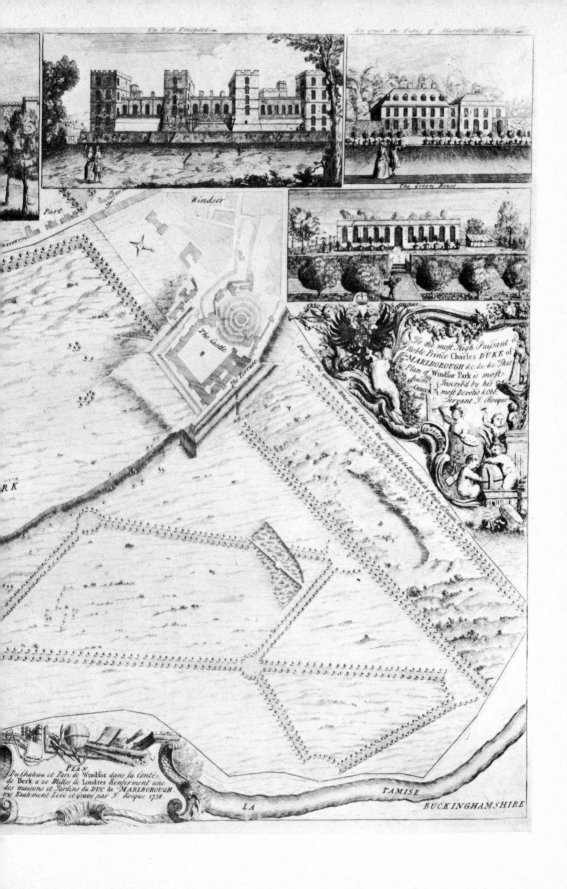

The green House.

Part of Windsor

The Castle

The Terrace

To the most High Puissant & Noble Prince Charles DUKE of MARLBOROUGH &c. &c. &c. This Plan of Windsor Park is most Inscrib'd by his Graces most Devoted & Obt. Servant I. Rocque.

PLAN Du Chateau et Parc de Windsor dans la Conté de Berk a 20 Miles de Londres Renferment une des maisons et Jardins du DUC de MARLBOROUGH &c. Exactement Levé et gravé par I. Rocque 1738.

LA TAMISE

BUCKINGHAMSHIRE

personal letters are addressed from there. In July 1702 there is a pretty cool one to the Dowager Electress of Hanover, Sophia, daughter of James I's daughter Elizabeth, and Prince Rupert's sister. Though an old lady, Sophia's ardent wish was to survive her sickly junior and be able to inscribe 'Queen of Great Britain' on her tomb. Queen Anne could not bear the family of Hanover, any more than Elizabeth I liked James of Scotland. Hence this missive from Windsor, July 1702: 'The thanks it has pleased you to give me regarding the insertion of your name in the Public Prayers of our Church are very obliging, and I too am very grateful. I considered this an indispensable act of good will towards the Person who, according to the Laws, is, after me, the Inheritor of the Crown.'

The tone is very different from her letter next summer, 1703, when Marlborough, frustrated in the Netherlands by his Dutch allies and at home by the extreme wings of both Tories and Whigs, threatened to retire. Anne: 'Give me leave to say you should a little consider your faithful friends and poor country, which must be ruined if ever you put your melancholy thoughts in execution. As for your poor, unfortunate, faithful Morley [herself], she could not bear it; for if ever you should forsake me, I would have nothing more to do with the world, but make another abdication. For what is a crown when the support of it is gone? [As her father had found]. I never will forsake your dear self, Mr Freeman nor Mr Montgomery [Marlborough and Godolphin], but always be your constant and faithful friend, and we four must never part till death mows us down with his impartial hand.'

Alas, for the deceptions of politics! These eloquent sentiments lasted only for the next year or two.

Marlborough's victory of Blenheim in 1704 – the greatest feat ever of English generalship in the centre of Europe – ended all thoughts of his retirement. The tradition is that the Queen was sitting with Prince George, playing a game of dominoes in the bay overlooking the north terrace, when Colonel Parke brought the tremendous news. The gift on such an occasion to the messenger was 500 guineas; Colonel Parke asked instead a miniature of the Queen and – a generous woman – she added to it a thousand guineas.

For the Marlboroughs she could not do enough, the Duke had imparted such glory to her reign. She herself gave him the royal manor of Woodstock, 'to be holden as of the castle of Windsor by fealty', the Duke and his descendants to render a white silk flag every year, with three fleurs-de-lys, on the anniversary of Blenheim. The custom is still kept up: one sees the annual white standard above Marlborough's bust in the Queen's Guard Chamber.

Anne found more and more that, as Queen, she had more than she could put up with from the politicians, and from Sarah, who was constantly pressing the Whigs upon her. At Windsor she felt freer from pressure than at St James's and could think things out for herself. Here she is objecting to the Duke of Queensberry: 'he will expect to be taken into my Service, which is a thing I can never consent to, his last tricking behaviour having made him more odious to me than ever.' Then, 'I cannot help venting my thoughts upon the Scotch affairs ... I think those people use me very hardly in opposing Lord Forfar's being of the Treasury.' Next month, she takes up her stand: 'I must own I dread the falling into the hands of either party, and the Whigs have had so many favours shown them of late that I fear a very few more will put me insensibly into their power. I know my dear unkind friend has so good an opinion of all that party that she will use all her endeavour ... to put one of them into this great post.'

One sees that Anne was by no means a cipher in government; she was in fact the source of authority and power. One sees also the ominousness in the phrase 'my dear unkind friend', though Sarah, the cleverer woman, did not. Next summer, 1706, the Queen was hoping for an end to the war: 'I having no ambition after the King of Spain is settled on his throne but to see an honourable peace, that – whenever it pleases God I shall die – I may have the satisfaction of leaving my poor country and all my friends in peace and quiet.' Alas, there was no prospect of peace: in 1703 she had given her one magnificent state entertainment to the Habsburg candidate for the throne of Spain – the trouble was that Spain wouldn't have him. Now she is nominating the Commissioners to settle the Union with Scotland – and writing to Sarah, 'now that you are come hither again, I hope you will not go to Woodstock without giving me one look, for whatever hard thoughts you may have of me, I am sure I do not deserve them; for though you are never so unkind, I will ever preserve a most sincere and tender passion for my dear Mrs Freeman'.

One perceives that this was a feminine way of putting herself in the right upon the end of any real friendship; her affections were now fixed upon Sarah's cousin, Abigail Hill, for whom the Queen found a marriage and a peerage for the husband: Lord and Lady Masham. In October 1709 she is writing to the Duke: 'You seem to be dissatisfied with my behaviour to the Duchess of Marlborough. I do not love complaining, but it is impossible to help saying on this occasion I believe nobody was ever so used by a friend as I have been by her ever since my coming to the Crown. I desire nothing but that she would leave off teasing and tormenting me, and behave herself with the decency she ought both to her friend and Queen, and this I hope you will make her do.'

Unfortunately Marlborough, who could do wonders with armies, could do nothing with Sarah. She said some very unseemly things about Anne's bringing her sick husband, in his last summer at Windsor, to 'the hot small house which

Jonathan Swift. 'Perhaps his was the greatest as it was the most
tormented spirit ever to appear upon the Windsor scene.'

made Prince George pant for breath', so that Mrs Masham could introduce political callers privately from the garden. The plain fact was that the country was weary of the war to which there seemed no end. It was the Queen's duty to interpret the nation's will towards peace; this coincided strongly with her own inclinations. It necessitated a drastic change of ministry, her turning to the Tories – and Mrs Masham's introducing Mr Harley by the back door.

The change of ministry in England, the undermining of the Duke of Marlborough, were matters of European importance, and of extreme difficulty: it took three years to bring about the Peace of Utrecht. In this struggle literary propaganda was a foremost weapon, and Harley recruited to his aid the genius of Swift. Perhaps his was the greatest, as it was the most tormented, spirit ever to appear upon the Windsor scene; there was at the same time something irresistible about him. We may take his contributions to Windsor literature as the most striking, the most memorable – and at the same time the meanest.

In July 1711 Swift was first taken down by Harley to Windsor for the night:

> And Harley, not ashamed his choice to own,
> Takes him to Windsor in his coach, alone.

Next week the Secretary of State, St John, carried him down and Swift remained there a fortnight, in a prebendary's house, writing a pamphlet for the ministry:

> At Windsor Swift no sooner can appear
> But St John comes and whispers in his ear;
> The waiters stand in ranks, the Yeomen cry
> 'Make room', as if a duke were passing by.

To Stella, away in Dublin, Swift bares his soul. He had had to borrow one of the Secretary's shirts to go unexpectedly to Court in. 'I generally am acquainted with about thirty in the Drawing-Room, and I am so proud I make all the lords come up to me. One passes half an hour pleasant enough. We had a dunce to preach before the Queen today, which often happens.' Himself, a man of genius, was never asked: too uncomfortable for the fools he thought them all. Conscious of his powers, he had been kept out all his life: in time he would take an almighty revenge. All the same, it is pathetic to see such a spirit reduced to boasting of his acquaintance with miserable peers no-one remembers now, except in so far as they crossed his path – and to understand why it was.

That fortnight the Queen was well enough: she was 'abroad today in order to hunt, but finding it disposed to rain, she kept in her coach. She hunts in a chaise with one horse, which she drives herself, and drives furiously, like Jehu, and is a mighty hunter, like Nimrod.' Next day, 'the Queen and I were going to take the air this afternoon, but not together; and were both hindered by a sudden rain. Her coaches and chaises all went back, and the guards too; and I scoured into the market place for shelter. I intended to have walked up the finest avenue I ever saw, two miles long, with two rows of elms on each side. [It is only in our time that these trees came to an end, and the avenue was replanted.] I walked in the evening a little upon the Terrace.'

Swift became very friendly with Mrs Masham, and sometimes supped with the couple; but close as his contact was, the writer who was the greatest ornament of her reign was never presented to the Queen, nor would she ever give any preferment in England to the author of *A Tale of a Tub*.

At Windsor Swift had more leisure for writing – and not only on behalf of the ministry, as we shall see. On 7 August, 'the Queen was hunting the stag till four this afternoon, and she drove in her chaise above forty miles; it was five before we went to dinner. Here are fine walks about this town. I sometimes walk up the Avenue.' Next day there was 'a Drawing-room at Court; but so few company that the Queen sent for us into her bedchamber, where we made our bows, and stood about twenty of us round the room; while she looked at us round, with her fan in her mouth, and once a minute said about three words to some that were nearest her, and then she was told dinner was ready, and went out'. So close – and there was still no presentation: she knew well enough who he was.

That is exactly how Sarah described Anne in her Memoirs; a woman of no intellectual interests whatever, she had absolutely no conversation – this was what Sarah found so unutterably tedious in attendance upon her, and left the duty to Abigail. A day or two later there was to be 'a famous horse-race' – perhaps the Datchet Plate started by her uncle, Charles II. 'We met the Queen coming back, and Miss Forester stood, like us with her hat off, while the Queen went by.'

Next week she was indicting her charge to the Archbishop of Canterbury for 'the promoting and encouraging Piety among our subjects, by such means as you shall judge to be most effectual for these purposes'. Then she was laid low by the gout: to Harley, promoted Earl of Oxford, 'I have been in so much pain all the last night and this day that it is not easy to me now to write.' In September, 'I think the Duke of Marlborough shows plainer than ever by this new project his unwillingness for a peace; but I hope our negotiations will succeed, and then it will not be in his power to prevent it.' Again and again she writes to Oxford, 'I have this business of the Peace so much at heart'; sometimes in pain, or in haste, 'I hope you will excuse the blots of this letter, for I am in haste and cannot write it over again.' Then in October came her proclamation for 'the Suppression of Vice by a faithful and impartial execution

Right: The Duchess of Somerset, the subject of Swift's poem, 'The Windsor Prophecy'.

of all Our Laws, which are now in force against Irreligion, Blasphemy, Profane Swearing and Cursing, Profanation of the Lord's Day, Excessive Drinking, Gaming, Lewdness, and all other dissolute, immoral and disorderly practices'.

It was all very unlike the domestic life of her uncle, Charles II, or even her dear father: a reaction from those bad old days had set in. And yet there was a memento of what they had been close beside her, in her friend the red-headed Duchess of Somerset, who had succeeded to Sarah's gold key as Mistress of the Robes. This great lady, the Percy heiress, had had a chequered and questionable matrimonial career, which had made a notorious scandal in her youth. She had married Tom Thynne of Longleat, Tom of Ten Thousand – a previous husband having died within a year of marrying her. But now the bride found

she could not fancy Tom Thynne, so she absconded to the Hague. A celebrated and very virile adventurer, Count Königsmarck, was enamoured of her, or at least a rival suitor; he arranged for the shooting of her husband in his coach, which is depicted in the well-known relief upon his tomb in Westminster Abbey. She thereupon married the Duke of Somerset.

This was the lady who now had the ear of the Queen, and dared to whisper her moral objections to Swift's preferment in the Church. This was what she got for her impertinence: the poem was dressed up in pseudo-medieval language, in bogus black-letter, and pretended to have been found in a Poor Knight's coffer in the cloisters. 'The Windsor Prophecy' is the most terrible of the poems Swift ever wrote, brilliant and envenomed: I cite only the description of the Duchess, underlining the references to her notorious past.

> And dear England, if aught I understand,
> Beware of *Carrots* from *Northumberland*.
> *Carrots* sown *Thynne* a deep root may get,
> If so they be in *Somer set*:
> Their *connings mark* thou, for I have been told,
> They assassin when young, and poison when old.
> Root out these *Carrots*, O thou whose name
> Is backwards and forwards always the same;
>   [i.e. Anna]
> And keep close to thee always that name
> Which backwards and forwards is almost the same
>   [i.e. Masham].
> And England wouldst thou be happy still,
> Bury those *Carrots* under a *Hill*.

As we have seen Mrs Masham's maiden name was Hill; she besought Swift to suppress the broadside for fear of angering the Queen. It had already got abroad, however; it is astonishing that Swift should have thought a bishopric possible after that, for all his services to the Tories and the cause of peace.

In September he spent every weekend at Windsor and the third and fifth weeks, colloguing with the Secretary of State about the pamphlet-warfare he was waging for the Tories – himself, like Oxford, a Whig by origin – and dining with the grandees at Lord Peterborough's house. He had 'left it and his gardens to the Secretary during his absence'. Peterborough had won fame fighting in Spain. 'It is the finest garden I have ever seen about this town, and abundance of hot walls for grapes, where they are in great plenty, and ripening fast.' The Castle at this time had acres of gardens on the southern slopes, as well as some on the northern. 'The Queen has the gout, and did not come to chapel, nor stir out from her chamber, but received the sacrament there, as she always does the first Sunday of the month. Yet we had a great Court ... The bishop of Bristol, who is Dean of Windsor, officiated last night at the cathedral. This they do to be popular, and it pleases mightily.'

Next day was held a Council, at which the Bishop was made a privy councillor and Lord Privy Seal– the last cleric to be so. One sees how far the Anglican tide had gone; but it did not carry that very un-Anglican cleric, Swift, any further up the beach. As he wrote:

> Swift had the sin of wit, no venial crime,
> Nay, 'twas affirmed he sometimes dealt in rhyme;
> Humour and mirth had place in all he writ:
> He reconciled divinity and wit.
> He moved, and bowed, and talked with too much grace,
> Nor showed the parson in his gait or face,
> Despised luxurious wines and costly meat,
> Yet still was at the tables of the great,
> Frequented lords, *saw those that saw the Queen.*

Actually, he detested the magnificent public tables kept at Windsor on Sundays, and preferred the intimate gatherings with the Lord Treasurer and Secretary and a few members of their private club, intelligent men like Sir William Windham and George Granville the Polite, later Lord Lansdowne. Even so, abstemious and possessed with his own thoughts, he loathed their long sittings and all the drink. To Stella he confided, 'I hate these suppers mortally; but I seldom eat anything.' Meanwhile, the Peace was going forward, the cause of which he did so much to advance with his famous tract, *The Conduct of the Allies*; 'and the Queen is in mighty good humour'. She was not at chapel, 'all for the better, for we had a dunce to preach' – yet another.

Instead of attending an evening assembly, 'I cooled my heels in the Cloisters till nine, then went in to the music meeting, where I had been often desired to go; but was weary in half an hour of their fine stuff, and stole out so privately that everybody saw me.' Or again, after dining with 'honest Colonel Godfrey' (Arabella Churchill's husband), he would walk on the Terrace, alone with his thoughts: the conjured spirit. 'But it grows bloody cold, and I have no waistcoat here.' Before leaving Windsor 'Lady Oglethorpe brought me and the Duchess of Hamilton together today in the Drawing-Room, and I have given her some encouragement, but not much'. He boasted to Stella, the Lord Keeper had said 'Dr Swift is not only all our favourite but our governor'. The Doctor left Windsor alone with the Lord Treasurer in his coach. But the Lord Treasurer could get him no reward for his transcendent services.

It was all the more provoking that he had fallen for its charms: summer, 1712, 'Windsor is a most delightful place. My lodgings there look upon Eton and the Thames; I wish I were owner of them: they belong to a prebend.' Swift puts this into verse in a poem on his favour with Oxford:

> My Lord would carry on the jest,
> And down to Windsor takes his guest.
> Swift much admires the place and air,
> And longs to be a canon there,
> In summer round the Park to ride,
> In winter – never to reside.
> 'A canon! that's a place too mean:
> No, Doctor, you shall be a Dean,
> Two dozen canons round your stall,
> And you the tyrant o'er them all.'

But there was no deanery, canonry, or prebend for him in England.

Now a new interest had come into his life: the intelligent and too responsive girl he called Vanessa. This summer he is writing to her, in the same pathetic strain in which he exhibited his inflamed sense of inferiority and resentment at his lot, that he had been at the Duchess of Shrewsbury's ball, 'looking a little singular among so many fine ladies and gentlemen'. However, the famous Doctor was more recognizable than they. He asked all Vanessa's family down for a few days, to see him in his power and glory. Vanessa proposed to come alone, with only her brother as escort. Swift did not reply to this, but sent a haunch of venison to her mother. 'I am full of business and ill humour.'

Swift was beginning on the book that was to become *The History of the Last Four Years of the Reign of Queen Anne* – he would like the post of Historiographer Royal, if nothing else (it went to a dull researcher). He was working overtime to prevent the ministry from breaking up, his grand friends were quarrelling bitterly, Oxford and St John, now Bolingbroke, at daggers drawn, Oxford drinking, Bolingbroke embezzling and conspiring. What idiots human were! From the Castle he wrote, 'one is kept constantly out of humour by a thousand unaccountable things in public proceedings, and when I reason with some friends, we cannot conceive how affairs can last as they are. I am again endeavouring, as I was last year, to keep people from breaking to pieces upon a hundred misunderstandings. One cannot withhold them from drawing different ways, while the enemy is watching to destroy both.' Nor was the Peace safely concluded even yet.

Meanwhile the Queen's health was precarious; when she fell ill and her physicians were fetched from London, 'you never saw such countenances as we all had, such dismal melancholy'. For they all knew that they depended on her – their jobs would not outlast her life; and Swift himself was not provided for. In the intervals of growing ill-health the Queen attended to business. In October she was contemplating a Chapter of the Garter, but 'I desire my intentions may yet be kept a secret.' In November the Duke of Ormonde is here: 'he comes of a solicitious family, therefore care must be taken that he makes no unreasonable requests'. In reply to a letter from the ever-living Louis xiv in the interests of her brother, James Edward – of whom she had written at the time of his birth, 'God knows whether he may be our brother' – she writes that she will do what is in her power at the peace-negotiations on his behalf. 'I do not at all doubt that he himself is fully convinced of it. I again repeat, Monsieur my Brother, that the consideration of your friendship will be a very prevailing motive to engage me anew in his interest, and in the interest of his Family, as occasion shall offer, for the future.' This did not amount to very much.

At last, in 1713, the Peace of Utrecht was concluded, and hailed in a poem by Swift's young friend, Pope: 'Windsor Forest'. The most precocious of poets, Pope had written the first part of it some years before. Even Wordsworth approved the touches of nature this celebrated, if youthful, poem contains:

> Here hills and vales, the woodland and the plain,
> Here earth and water seem to strive again;
> Not chaos-like together crushed and bruised,
> But, as the world, harmoniously confused:
> Where order in variety we see,
> And where, though all things differ, all agree.
> Here waving groves a chequered scene display
> And part admit, and part exclude, the day . . .
> There interspersed in lawns and opening glades
> Thin trees arise that shun each other's shades.
> Here in full light the russet plains extend:
> There wrapped in clouds the blueish hills ascend.
> Ev'n the wild heath displays her purple dyes,
> And midst the desert fruitful fields arise,
> That crowned with tufted trees and springing corn,
> Like verdant isles the sable waste adorn.

Critics have been right to see in this piece, from the prime classical poet of the succeeding age, a foretaste, along with Gray, of the Romantic Movement.

From this Pope goes on to depict the contrast between Augustan civilisation and the barbarism of old Norman days:

> Not thus the land appeared in ages past,
> A dreary desert and a gloomy waste,
> To savage beasts and savage laws a prey,
> And kings more furious and severe than they.

But now Anne reigned, a huntress whom the Tory poet compares with Diana, for all the improbable contrast of figure:

> Nor envy, Windsor, since thy shades have seen
> As bright a goddess, and as chaste a queen;
> Whose care, like hers, protects the sylvan reign,
> The earth's fair light and empress of the main.

Now the empress's fleets had won victory at last against the tyrant Louis xiv, and the poet took up his pen to complete the work and celebrate the Peace in a more lofty strain. He dedicated the poem to the Tory Lord Lansdowne, grandson of the gallant Sir Bevil Grenville, killed at Lansdowne in the Civil War. The poet recited more recent events in Windsor's history:

> Surrey, the Granville of a former age;

Edward iii and the institution of the Garter depicted in St George's Hall:

> Then from her roofs when Verrio's colours fall
> And leave inanimate the naked wall,
> Still in thy song should vanquished France appear,
> And bleed for ever under Britain's spear.

Windsor's special heroes are cited, 'ill-fated Henry', and Charles i:

> Make sacred Charles's tomb for ever known,
> (Obscure the place, and uninscribed the stone).

The Civil War receives its proper condemnation:

> A dreadful series of intestine wars,
> Inglorious triumphs and dishonest scars.

The Augustan age of Anne had brought them to an end:

> At length great Anna said – 'Let discord cease!'
> She said, the world obeyed, and all was peace!

Peace was achieved abroad before she died, the political discord at home increased – but at least it expressed itself in the form of party political conflict, not civil war. The Queen's troubles now were with her own government: she felt herself subjected to intolerable pressure from the Tories. She wrote to Oxford: 'you cannot wonder that I, who have been ill used so many years, should desire to keep myself from being again enslaved. And if must always comply and not be complied with is [sic], I think, very hard and what I cannot submit to.' Next summer at Windsor Swift saw her looking 'in very good health, which she finds there more than anywhere else'. From a reference back, reminding Vanessa of it, it appears that she had after all paid him a visit there the year before. From the Queen's last communications with Oxford we see that his government was breaking up. 'Now that I have a pen in my hand I cannot help desiring you again when you come next, to speak plainly, lay everything open and hide nothing from me, or else how is it possible I can judge of anything?' She complained at the end that he came to her drunk, that he could not explain the business, nor she understand what he said. In the last days of her life she dismissed him and changed her government; but the struggle was too much for her: on 1 August 1714 Queen Anne was dead.

Before losing power Oxford had done the best he could for Swift: he could get no more than a deanery, and that out of the country, in mad Ireland. From the new Dean of St Patrick's the Queen received her eternal reward:

> By an old redhaired, murdering hag pursued,
> A crazy prelate [i.e. Archbishop Sharp], and
> a Royal Prude,
> By dull divines, who look with envious eyes
> On every genius that attempts to rise,
> And, pausing o'er a pipe, with doubtful nod,
> Give hints that poets ne'er believe in God . . .
> Now Madam Coningsmark her vengeance vows
> On Swift's reproaches for her murdered spouse,
> From her red locks her mouth with venom fills,
> And thence into the royal ear instils.
> The Queen incensed, his services forgot,
> Leaves him a victim to the vengeful Scot . . .

In truth, one could not offend Jonathan Swift with impunity.

Old Mrs Delany, friend of George III and Queen Charlotte,
who established her at Windsor.

5
Hanoverian Neglect; Georgian Domesticity

FTER Queen Anne's death the Castle entered upon a long decline, a period of desuetude. The Hanovarians, accustomed to the mud-flats of northern Germany, preferred St James's, Kensington and Hampton Court. In the first two decades George I and George II came down occasionally, but after the 1730's they left the Duke of Cumberland as Ranger of the Forest to take the lead there.

The Tory crash in 1714 began the long Whig ascendency, and with it the poets changed their tune. Sarah Marlborough's son-in-law, Sunderland, whom she pressed on Queen Anne – the Queen detested this Whig doctrinaire – now emerged as a leading figure in the government of George I. Thomas Tickell, Addison's friend, addressed an attractive Ode to him at Windsor in 1720.

> Thou dome, where Edward first enrolled
> His red-cross knights and barons bold,
> Whose vacant seats, by virtue bought,
> Ambitious emperors have sought:
> Where Britain's foremost names are found,
> In peace beloved, in war renowned . . .
> Once more a Spencer waits,
> A name familiar to thy gates,
> Sprung from the chief whose prowess gained
> The Garter while thy founder reigned.

Not only are the flower of medieval chivalry cited but recent politic recruits:

> But on just law-givers bestowed,
> These emblems Cecil did invest,
> And gleamed on wise Godolphin's breast.

It is pleasant, as it is rare, to see these figures rather outside the Tory Pantheon celebrated, with the end of the Stuarts.

Next year we find Lady Lechmere surprised that the new king 'should not choose to be there sometimes: it has so much more the air of a palace than his house here – the Park's so beautiful there, and Hyde Park here, at his garden gate, so shamefully kept'. In the Drawing-Room at Windsor there met one day three shades of the historic past, who could evoke so many memories: the Duchess of Portsmouth, Lady Orkney and Lady Dorchester. Said the last, 'Heavens! who would have thought that we three royal whores should meet here!' The first had been Charles II's mistress, the second William III's, she herself, better known as Catherine Sedley, James II's. Perhaps they met under the eye of the awful Melusine Schulenberg, George I's, whom he made Duchess of Kendal.

A lady made of different stuff, who became celebrated as Mrs Delany – it was a *marriage blanche* – was a niece of the Jacobite Lord Lansdowne (who spent the years 1715–17 in the Tower). Her uncle had found for her a promising marriage to a well-off yokel of a Cornish squire, Pendarves, which she should have made the most of. But, as the bluestocking Mrs Montagu said, her friend would never commit the *grossièreté* of having a child. Poor Pendarves took a house at Windsor to please his aristocratic young bride; it looked out over Little Park, and early in the morning the young woman would walk there. The Hanoverian ambassador fancied her; the horrible Schulenberg set him on her track, told him where to find her and encouraged him to follow. When he did so, there was a scene of outraged virtue: she threatened to go up to the windows where the Hanoverian king sat after dinner and denounce the ambassador. Whether she would have found much delicacy of sympathy is another question; but her chastity alone was invincible.

George II's Court came down for St George's feast in 1730 and stayed on for hunting and horse-racing. Clever Lord Hervey, Vice-Chamberlain of the Household, describes the entertainments to his beloved Stephen Fox.

> I was yesterday from seven o'clock in the morning till two this morning constantly upon my legs, excepting half an hour that I was at dinner, and about an hour that I lay down in the afternoon. To compensate for which trouble I had the recreation of seeing one set of performers bowing till their backs ached four hours in the morning; another set eating till they spewed and drinking till they reeled at noon; and a third dancing and sweating till they were ready to drop at night.

The brilliant Hervey was a fastidious man – for which they called him a pansy. There was, of course, something in it. He writes to his Stephen, 'you are as much present in my mind as if I had seen you but this morning; and yet it seems as long as if I had not seen you these seven years'.

During the next month Hervey wrote frequently to him, but the Victorian Lord Ilchester chose only a few letters that might be printed. In August:

what are the Royal pleasures you talk of, my dear Ste., which are not given equally to every subject? Do the trappings of Royalty make the amusements of the country more agreeable? Are our chaises or our boats safer for being gilt? Is the air sweeter for a Court; or the walks pleasanter for being bounded with sentinels? What entertainment does Windsor afford that cannot be found at Redlynch? But transpose that question, and I should quickly answer – the greatest joy I ever did or can know.

Hervey informs his friend that all the news at Windsor, 'every whisper and consultation', is of the ferocious treatment of the Prince of Prussia (to become Frederick the Great) by his father, so that the young man had tried to run away. The Hohenzollern King had thereupon imprisoned his son and his accomplices – and was to execute his too intimate friend. The quarrels between George II and *his* son Frederick, though shocking enough, were nothing compared with this – perhaps the English climate mollified them. (However, George I, as Elector of Hanover, had imprisoned his wife, George II's mother, for life.)

At the end of August the Court at Windsor was astonished to hear of the King of Sardinia's abdication, out of pure affection for *his* son. 'About nine o'clock last night, whilst we were at play in the King's private apartment, the Duke of Newcastle came in, like Prince Guicomar, "haste in his steps and wonder in his eye" ... with this piece of news.' Early in September Hervey had had to bustle off to a royal party in London: 'the bustle of yesterday, getting up by five o'clock and sitting up till past two, has half killed me ... I have lain abed most part of this day, and am this moment stepping into the coach to return to Windsor.' A few days later: 'there is no part of my time I repine so much at not being master of as the hours I wish to dedicate to you. The King is this moment come from a horse-race, where popularity, I believe, carried him, as it does a-stag-hunting. For sure the pleasures of both entertainments were calculated for such better eyes than his Majesty's.' No man is a hero to his own valet: one sees that these royals had no terrors for their Vice-Chamberlain.

A couple of days later, 'I have been hunting all this morning with the King in the worst country, the worst weather, and with the worst dogs, that ever poor sportsmen were cursed with. I fancy the King says to himself every hunting morning, "Take physic pomp" [sic] as the King does in *Hamlet*, and has put himself into a course of these Royal medicines for the good of his body politic.' One must remember that these Hanoverians were extremely unpopular – and indeed, like the Germans they were, they had no charm. The King had felt it incumbent upon him to return from the horse-race 'wet to the skin in an open chaise, whilst we *chickens* of his suite chose the ignoble safety of a dry coach with glasses up'.

Hervey saw a good deal of Lord and Lady Bateman, old Sarah Marlborough's favourite dislike among her daughters. 'I dine there, they dine here; they hunt with us in the morning, play with us at night, and seem to take very kindly to the Court.' The inwardness of this was that Lord Bateman was a Tory – another reason for the Duchess's dislike. 'The Prince [Frederick] is most particularly civil to them. Old Marlborough is come to the Lodge, and lets Lady Di. sometimes be of the party.' This was her charming granddaughter Lady Diana Spencer, and what the ambitious old creature was up to was to marry her to the Prince of Wales, settling £100,000 upon her to bring it off.* It did not work.

A fortnight later the Court was still at Windsor.

We jog on here *le vieux train*. A little walking, a little hunting and a little playing, a little flattering, a little railing and a little lying: a little hate, a little friendship, and a little love: a little hope and a little fear, a little joy and a little pain. They are the ingredients that compose the daily vicissitudes of Court meals, and – though some of them are rather hard of digestion – yet if one knows the quality and manages the quantity of them, I think, with some caution, not too nice a taste, and a good digestion, it is possible to live at such a table and escape both starving and surfeiting.

A couple of days later the beloved Ste. was coming to Windsor. 'Not that I will lend you for a moment of the day or night that I can have you.' Hervey was in waiting, so 'if I can so contrive that the hours you are not with me may not lie as heavy upon your hands as I always find those in which I can not be with you . . .' and he quotes Lady Mary Wortley-Montagu:

> In crowded Courts I find myself alone,
> And feel no commerce grateful but your own.

The nullity of such a life transpires, unless nerved by politics or elevated by the arts. Even Queen Anne, no aesthete, completed the work on the Grand Staircase by commissioning Thornhill to paint scenes from Ovid, the gardens were improved and a carriage road made through the Long Walk. The horrid Georges did nothing; George I was not ashamed to confess that he 'didn't like boetry and he didn't like bainting'.

This did not wholly discourage the Muses. The long stay of the Court described in Hervey's Letters resulted in the publication of *The Windsor Medley* of prose and verse. Pope's friend, the scholarly and religious Gilbert West, produced in 1740 a long poem on 'The Institution of the Order of the Garter'; described as a 'Dramatic Poem', it is anything but dramatic: it is more like a masque or a libretto for an opera, the scene 'Windsor Park, with a Prospect of the Castle'. Edward III, Queen Philippa, the Black Prince are attended by Spirits, Bards, Druids, the Genius of England; the evil genius appears to be King John.

---

* cf. my *The Early Churchills*, p. 387.

> Hither, all ye heavenly powers,
> From your empyreal bowers,
> From the fields for ever gay,
> From the star-paved milky way,
> From the moon's reluctant horn,
> From the star that wakes the morn . . .

Charming in its way, it is but sub-Milton:

> But lo! fair Windsor's towers appear,
>   And hills with spreading oaks embrowned;
> Hark! hark! the voice of joy I hear,
>   Sung by a thousand echoes round;
> And now I view a glittering train,
> In triumph march o'er yonder plain.
>
>   etc.

What a delightful world it was, when the country round really was vernal, as he says, and there was room to move round in it – the Augustan world in which all things were adjusted to the human scale, the mind could compass it and the imagination spread its wings!

West's friend, Pope, returned to those earlier scenes in the 'Lines Written in Windsor Forest':

> All hail, once pleasing, once inspiring shade!
>   Scene of my youthful loves and happier hours!
> Where the kind Muses met me as I strayed,
>   And gently pressed my hand and said, 'Be ours!' . . .

Another poet of the age, whose boyhood passed in this place, wrote less about it. In his 'Ode on a Distant Prospect of Eton College', Gray has only a salute for the view from it:

> And ye that from the stately brow
> Of Windsor's heights th'expanse below
> Of grove, of lawn, of mead survey,
> Whose turf, whose shade, whose flowers among
> Wanders the hoary Thames along
> His silver-winding way.

Brought up as they were on the classics, Horace Walpole wrote to Gray from Rome in 1740, 'our memory sees more than our eyes in this country. For realities Windsor or Richmond Hill is infinitely preferable to Albano or Frascati.' To

View of Eton College by Canaletto.

us brought up on English history Windsor, in addition to its natural beauty, has the added dimension of historic memories – the more poignant because now overlaid, threatened, engulfed.

From the 1740's the Castle gradually fell into a state of romantic decay – just the place for Horace Walpole, who made such a cult of it. In the summer of 1746 he is writing to his lazy, inattentive chum of Eton days, George Montagu, 'if you can find me out any clean, little house in Windsor, ready furnished that is not absolutely in the middle of the town, but near you, I shall be glad to take it for three or four months'. Marshal Bellisle, 'so ambitious and intriguing a man, who was author of this whole war', had been captured in the course of it and sent down to Windsor on parole. 'He was at first kept magnificently close, but the expense proving above £100 per day', he was expedited to Nottingham, like Marshal Tallard after Blenheim. Bellisle, who had very grand ideas of his own importance, had taken Frogmore House.

Horace Walpole was contented with his little house within the precincts at £40 a year. 'Furniture I find I have in abundance, which I shall send down immediately; but shall not be able to be at Windsor at the quivering dame's before tomorrow se'nnight.' He wanted to remain in London for the execution of the Jacobite lords of the '45 rebellion, of which he has left us such brilliant accounts. After this he took up his residence, writing to Horace Mann in Florence, 'I am retired hither like an old summer dowager; only that I have no toad-eater to take the air with me in the back part of my lozenge-coach, and to be scolded. [Dowagers and maiden-ladies bore their arms within a lozenge.] I propose spending the greatest part of every week here till the Parliament meets.'

He was still there in October, he liked it so much. He wrote to his cousin Conway in Paris, comparing himself to Diogenes in his tub; if only the uncouth and lumbering Duke of Cumberland, whom he preferred however to Alexander the Great,

and who certainly can intercept more sunshine, would stand out of my way, which he is extremely in, while he lives in the Park here, I should love my little tub of £40 a year more than my palace *dans la rue des ministres* [i.e. Arlington Street], with all my pictures and bronzes, which you ridiculously imagine I have encumbered myself with in my solitude. Solitude it is, as to the tub itself, for no soul lives in it with me. But George Montagu lives but two barrels off; and Ashton lives at the foot of that hill which you mention with a melancholy satisfaction that always attends the reflection.

They had all been boys at Eton together; here were their friendships for life formed; they could not but look back on those days with nostalgia, for

Horace Walpole at Strawberry Hill.

they meant youth, and innocence, and hope. Thinking of it, Horace enclosed Gray's Ode, which enshrined it all.

Next summer Walpole is writing from Arlington Street, amid the bustle of Parliament – for he was a Member – 'you will think I have removed my philosophy [i.e. Diogenes'] from Windsor with my tea-things'. But he faithfully forwards news of the doings of the mountainous Keeper there. This was William Augustus, George II's militarist son, who was most unpopular for the Teutonic brutality of his repression of the Highlanders in the '45. The year after he took up residence. Horace did not fail to record it: 'The Duke of Cumberland is here at his Lodge with three whores and three *aide-de-camps* and the country swarms with people. He goes to races and they make a ring about him as at a bear-baiting.'

A year or two later, 'his savage temper increases every day'. A poor young soldier had been court-martialled for counterfeiting leave for only a day.

They ordered him two hundred lashes; but Nolkejumskoi, who loves blood like a leech, insisted it was not enough – has made them sit three times and swears they shall sit these sick months till they increase the punishment. The fair Mrs Pitt has been mobbed in the Park, and with difficulty rescued by some gentlemen, only because this bashaw is in love with her. [She was an actress.] You heard, I suppose, of his other amour with the Savoyard girl. He sent her to Windsor and offered her £100, which she refused because he was a heretic; he sent her back on foot.

These Hanoverians were as mean as they were vulgar.

However, the Duke was a man of parts. He greatly improved his Ranger's Lodge in the Great Park, and extended its area by a large enclosure of waste land in the parish of Egham – which he then walled round – 'and without making any compensation to the parish'. When Holbein's Gate at Whitehall was demolished, he intended to re-erect it as the terminus of the Long Walk. This good idea was prevented by a stroke. He had been disgraced by his peppery father, for the unfavourable Convention of Closterseven he had signed, by which the Hanoverian army laid down its arms. When he re-appeared at Court, George II said, 'here is my son who has ruined me and disgraced himself'. Horace Walpole described him at the end, 'he had grown enormously fat, had completely lost the use of one eye, and saw but imperfectly with the other'. However, it appears that the wits were unfair to him: the family made good butts for English writers, then and thereafter – Thackeray, for example; and the Holbein Gate would have been a good idea: instead, we have a monstrous equestrian statue of George III.

George III was the first member of his family to speak English like an Englishman, and he was anxious to disengage himself, as far as possible, from the Hanoverian past. It was probably one of his unspoken reasons for his extra-ordinary kindness and attention to old Mrs Delany, establishing her in a house at Windsor, making a favourite of her, his family visiting her every day. For the Hanoverians had something of an inferiority-complex about the senior line they had displaced – and Mrs Delany was a living link with all that Stuart past. Her grandfather, Bernard Granville, had been the messenger to Charles II to assure him of his restoration; her father had been a dependant of Queen Anne's Court, she herself brought up as a girl at Whitehall, with the Queen's promise of a post as maid-of-honour. Her family had never recovered from the Stuart disaster.

Meanwhile, during the years of neglect, Walpole occasionally notes a piece of Windsor news. In 1750 the housekeeper of the Castle is dead, 'an old monster that Verrio painted for one of the Furies'. Next year we hear that the admirable and Reverend Walter Harte, author of an excellent *History of Gustavus Adolphus* and other works, 'has taken possession of his prebendal house, which is a very pretty one'. Horace, like the connoisseur he was, had a remarkable visual memory. In 1762 he is recalling the celebrated portrait of Venetia Digby – still there – and 'what treasures there are in private seats, if one knew where to hunt them'. Alas! In 1764 he is regretting that 'I have never been able to per-suade any to engrave the Beauties at Windsor, which are daily perishing for want of fires in that palace. Most of them entered into a plan I had undertaken for an edition of Grammont with portraits.' It proved too expensive, but what a treasure of a book, with fine eighteenth-century engravings, we have thereby lost!

While Charles II's royal apartments mouldered and Verrio's frescoes perished from damp, other Stuart descendants were given 'grace and favour' residence in other parts of the Castle. There was Horace Walpole's niece, the beautiful young widow of the second Earl Waldegrave – James II's great-grandson. This lady kept her name, though secretly married to George III's brother, the Duke of Gloucester. Her situation was so equivocal that people suggested to Horace, who had written an absurd *jeu d'esprit, Historic Doubts* about Richard III, that he might as well write another about another Gloucester. Eton boys crowded up the hill to gaze upon the mysterious beauty, 'Lady Waldegrave at Castle prayers.' Her three Waldegrave daughters were given lodgings in the Castle. The later Hanoverians were given to picking up Stuart relics.

At last in the 1770's George III saw an opportunity to live at Windsor, though the Royal Apartments were by now uninhabitable. In 1775 the house Queen Anne had occupied on the south side, looking up against the Castle, became vacant. George III got Sir William Chambers to add on a long, excessively plain, wing; still it was not large enough to accommodate his numerous daughters. Two years later Queen Charlotte bought Nell Gwyn's house from her ducal descendant and fitted it up for the youngest of the six royal virgins. Chambers advised that the Castle could be rendered habitable only at enormous expense, so George III contented himself with undertaking repairs at first, then commissioning the restoration of St George's Chapel. By 1786 he had brought the state apartments back into commission; in 1804 the royal family moved into the Castle, though Queen Charlotte could not bear the cold and the inconvenience of it. Further work was stopped by the King's mental breakdown – when he was confined to the rooms on the North Terrace, next to that where Queen Anne heard the news of Blenheim. All the same, it was George III who initiated the rehabilitation of the Castle; his son George IV who accomplished its transformation, as we see it today.

George III deferred work on the Castle until Chambers' death, perhaps feeling that he would be incapable of working in the Gothic idiom it demanded. Ultimately he found an architect in James Wyatt who could make the transition from classic to Gothic, as he had done from Chatsworth to Fonthill. Meanwhile the King found in Henry Emlyn a designer whose woodwork was extraordinarily effective in repairing and adding to the stalls in St George's Chapel. Woodwork, stonework, glass – all was in need of repair. The east window was replaced by an immense transparency of the Resurrection by the King's favourite painter, Benjamin West; some, including Miss Burney, were ecstatic about it at the time, but both Wyatt and Lysons, who had more sense of the past than West, who was American, regretted it. The Victorians couldn't bear it, and made away with it. George III, who inherited the Hanoverian love of music, and especially of Handel, presented a new organ. Altogether he spent some £14,000 on the Chapel, the canons raising the rest.

The King proposed to turn the disused eastern chapel into a Chapter house for the Order of the Garter. Wyatt removed Wolsey–Henry VIII's unfinished tomb; eventually it was decided to turn the place into a tomb-house, and a vast royal vault for the family was excavated beneath. Wyatt began Gothicising the upper ward; this had not gone far when the King's illness held up the intended programme. But it seems clear that Wyatville's work carried on along some of the lines previously indicated, in particular the obvious opening of a gate from the Long Walk into the upper ward, George IV's Gate.

Such was the background when the monarch returned to take up residence at Windsor, to the accompaniment of unkind comments from unbelieving old Whigs like Horace Walpole. This monarch was as respectable as he was religious. We find him writing,

Right: George III in his Windsor uniform.

George III and his family walking on the Terrace.
Nell Gwyn's house can be seen to the left of the
Queen's lodge.

Queen Charlotte in 1819 from a painting by Zoffany. She bought
Nell Gwyn's house at Windsor.

it is a desirable thing to me that the Deanery of Windsor should be in the hands of a respectable man, and as he is an officer of the Garter [Registrar] wish at least that his name should be of note. It has occurred to me that by removing the Bishop of Carlisle to the Deanery, which is £1000 p.a., Mr Pitt could then recommend to the residentiary of St Paul's, which is worth £800; the additional £200 the Bishop will get will just pay for a London house. I write my first thoughts to prevent applications; no-one has a guess of my intentions.

His first thoughts were much to the point, and very characteristic of him: the careful eye for detail, particularly of a financial nature, while a London house was useful for an episcopal supporter in the Lords.

The unregenerate Walpole, who appeared to be immortal – and in the event turned out to be so – is writing in 1779: 'The most pious of Princes, who, in the tumult of civil affairs [the American war was on], never neglects religion, has lately taken on him the dispensation of cathedral fees at Windsor, and endeavoured to put them on a new footing. But, as hornets love honey, though they do not make it, one of the canons withstands the Head of the Church and defends the property of Faith against the Defender.'

Nor did the Squire of Windsor, as the Whigs called him, see why he should not call the tune in the election of MPs like other squires with a borough at their gates. Admiral Keppel was a Whig and a pro-American, so he was thrown out at the election in 1780. The Marquis of Rockingham was '*grieved* that the Squire of Windsor prevailed against Admiral Keppel'. Horace Walpole was at first ironical about it: 'Though all the royal bakers and brewers and butchers voted against him, you must not imagine it was by mandate. His Majesty himself told the Admiral he hoped he would carry his election: how saucy in his servants to thwart his wishes!' In his next Horace comes clean: it transpired that the monarch had not been so magnanimous, nor his servants so disregardful: Keppel's throwing out was 'by the personal veto of the first inhabitant'. The report was that the King had said to a silk-mercer, in his staccato, psittacotic manner, 'The Queen wants a gown – wants a gown – No Keppel – No Keppel!'

His eldest sons, the Prince of Wales and Duke of York, took no pains to conceal their pleasure at Keppel's return for Surrey – such were the relations within the royal family; 'while Prince Augustus was locked up in the nursery for wearing the Admiral's colours'. But perhaps this was Whig romancing – if Whigs are capable of romancing. And the impartial historian reflects that it is useful for a royal family to have a foot in both camps.

Politics apart, Horace could not conceal his affection for the Castle, and eleven years later – he was indestructible – the old man gives us far the best appreciation of the new work being done.

I went with General Conway to visit one of my antediluvian passions – not a
Statira or Roxana, but one pre-existent to myself: one Windsor Castle. I was so
delighted and so juvenile that, without attending to anything but my eyes, I stood full
two hours and a half, and found that half my lameness consists in my indolence. Two
Berrys [the old gallant was writing to the two Miss Berrys], a Gothic chapel, and an
historic castle are anodynes to a torpid mind. I now fancy that old age was invented by
the lazy.

St George's Chapel, that I always worshipped, though so dark and black that I
could see nothing distinctly, is now being cleaned and decorated, a scene of lightness
and graces. Mr Conway was so struck with its Gothic beauties and taste that he owned
the Grecian style would not admit half the variety of its imagination. There is a new
screen prefixed to the choir, so airy and harmonious, that I concluded it Wyatt's; but
it is by a Windsor architect, whose name I forget [i.e. Emlyn].

Horace goes on to be comic about West's Resurrection, with Christ

scrambling to heaven in a fright and not ascending calmly in secure dignity, and
Judas below, so gigantic that he seems more likely to burst by his bulk than through
guilt . . . The Castle itself is smugged up, is better glazed, has got some new stools,
clocks, and looking glasses, much embroidery in silk, and a gaudy, clumsy throne,
with a medallion at top of the King's and Queen's heads, over their own – an odd kind
of tautology whenever they sit there! There are several tawdry pictures by West, of the
history of the Garter; but the figures are too small for that majestic place. However,
upon the whole, I was glad to see Windsor a little revived.

What a writer Horace Walpole was! And what a man of taste! Undoubtedly
he was right about West. It is ironic to think that, in their different ways and
though at opposite poles politically, both Walpole and George III advanced
the Gothic movement in taste. One sees the change foreshadowed in a comment
of bluestocking Mrs Damer to one of Walpole's Berrys: 'The Chapel is really
and to my surprise repaired with true taste, and beautiful. I hope you admire
Gothic. Gothic in the grand style quite turns my head whenever I see it.' The
Castle's grand revival was yet to come.

In September 1785 the King and Queen installed Mrs Delany at Windsor in
the kindest way possible. They placed a house at her disposal not fifty yards
from their own, where they could visit her every day, furnished it all with
stores complete, and gave her a pension of £300 a year. The King himself was
there to receive her with open arms. It all furnished Horace with material for
describing the reception of this old lady of eighty-five in terms of Louis XIV
receiving his last mistress, whom he secretly married.

Have you heard the history of our Madame de Maintenon? *There* I am of the best authority: I know many particulars from her own mouth. In short, *la Veuve* Delany, not Scarron, sent her woman to Windsor to get by heart the ichnography of the hotel granted to her . . . It was his Majesty's command that she should bring nothing down but her lady's clothes and the boxes of her maids, for Louis le Grand is very considerate: she must bring no plate, china, linen, wine etc.; all would be ready. Louis himself pointed out where Mlle. Daubigny [Mme de Maintenon's niece], the great-niece [actually Miss Port], should sleep. When the new favourite arrived, Louis himself was at the door to hand her out of the chaise; there ends my journal. Others say that after a short visit, *elle le renvoyait triste, mais jamais désespéré.*

This was what Mme de Maintenon had said, in her fine forties; Mrs Delany was in her eighties.

Queen Charlotte's welcome was no less warm. 'My dearest Mrs Delany, if coming to me will not fatigue your spirits too much I shall receive you with open arms, and am, your affectionate friend, Charlotte.' There Mrs Delany remained till her death three years later, respected, venerated by everyone; a lady of the highest breeding and, as talented as she was amusing, people made a cult of her – none more so than the royal family, for whom she was rather a catch with her old Jacobite lineage. She had a remarkable talent for cutting out and reproducing flowers in paper-mosaic – there must still be examples, possibly collections, of her dainty art in existence. The King gave orders that any rare plants in the royal gardens should be transmitted to her. The whole family at Windsor were very fond of her: the extraordinary consideration and delicacy with which they treated her make a charming chapter in the Windsor story.

The domestic interior of George and Charlotte is more fully documented than that of almost any royal pair, owing to the Queen's taking into her service Miss Burney, already well-known for her novels, *Cecilia* and *Evelina*. Little did they realise the risk, for the lady-novelist, frustrated in her literary life and missing the intellectual interests of Dr Burney's free-and-easy household, assiduously kept a Diary. When it was published in the first years of Victoria's reign, it was carefully pruned, and passages suppressed. Macaulay inherited the Whig prejudices against George III and his Court, and was too sympathetic to Miss Burney's complaints as to her situation. Lord Melbourne disagreed with him: 'It appears to Lord Melbourne that Miss Burney was well enough con-tented to live in the Palace and receive her salary, but that she was surprised and disgusted as soon as she found she was expected to give up some part of her time to conform to some rules and to perform some duty.'

Actually Miss Burney gives one a very favourable portrait of the Squire of Windsor, quite different from the Whig and American caricature of him: he was kind and considerate, a conscientious good man, quite generous enough without the weak, ill-considered extravagance of the Stuarts. (He came to the rescue of the last Stuart Pretender, Henry Benedict, Cardinal of York, with a pension that made his last years easy.) And George III, high-minded and decent, was a cultivated man: a connoisseur of music, fascinated by astronomy – he made the career of Sir William Herschel – he was one of the greatest book-collectors of his time: his wonderful library forms the nucleus of the British Museum. Little credit has the King received for these genuine accomplishments, but one sees through the eyes of Miss Burney what a nice man he really was, and deservedly popular. Her portrait of Queen Charlotte is rather too favourable: she was not as nice as she is painted, and Miss Burney's depiction here is tinged with sycophancy.

The real fly in the ointment was Miss Burney's official superior, Charlotte's old head waiting-woman, the Schwellenberg. Perhaps it was hard luck on her that the new recruit to the household was a novelist with a sharp eye and sharper pen, for the old German martinet, intolerable to put up with, was still a gift to a writer. Macaulay takes obvious pleasure in describing her: 'Mme Schwellenberg, a hateful old toad-eater, as illiterate as a chambermaid, as proud as a whole German Chapter, rude, peevish, unable to bear solitude, unable to conduct herself with common decency in society.' This is a bit harsh. Miss Burney may have been a bit pert, or the old creature may have noticed a look on the clever English girl's face. Even Miss Burney allowed that she was devoted to her mistress's interests and hadn't a bad heart; she was just a German.

It was Mrs Delany who had made this opening for her young friend, who had no prospects of her own in her father's home with an unsympathetic step-mother. Besides, with all the chances at Court, there might be a marriage for her. Mrs Delany was delighted, so was Dr Burney, everybody seemed pleased, except Miss Burney herself. Queen Charlotte 'received me with a most gracious bow of the head, and a smile that was all sweetness. She saw me much agitated, and attributed it, no doubt, to the awe of her presence.' But Miss Burney was not awed: 'O, she little knew my mind had no room in it for feelings of that sort!' Miss Burney was unfavourably impressed by the Germanness of it all. At table there was a German colonel who stopped speaking when a new dish appeared, 'to feast his eyes upon it, exclaim something in German, and suck the inside of his mouth'. Next day the sight of turtle on the table raised him to ecstasy. When the King bestowed on him some post in Hanover, 'he was as happy as if just casting his eyes upon pineapple, melon, and grapes'.

There was a great deal of music, private concerts in the Castle, and Charles Wesley to play Handel on the organ in Chapel. But there was always the Schwellenberg, presiding at the ladies-in-waiting tea-table for hours in the

Right: Fanny Burney, the famous novelist whose Diary gives an inside view of Queen Charlotte's household.

evening, with no conversation, never speaking English but from necessity, always on the look-out for some slight, in the German way, or some sign of insubordination in one who refused to be regarded as a subordinate. When the Queen presented Miss Burney, who was already quite well provided, with a gown, the Schwellenberg made the gift with such tact: 'the Queen says you are not rich – the Queen will give you a gown!' etc. The old creature, obsequious herself, expected that this 'would have been caught at with obvious avidity; but indeed she was mistaken'.

There was the tyranny of the tea-table: Miss Burney was expected to attend, but not to speak; if she absented herself, this was insubordination. When a

French lady, a friend of the novelist Mme de Genlis, was thrilled to meet the author of *Evelina*, the Schwellenberg was astonished: 'upon my word! You sorprise me!' Miss Burney took refuge in Mrs Delany: 'accustomed to place me herself so high, to see me now even studiously shunned had an effect upon her tender mind that gave me uneasiness to observe'. Miss Burney was all sensibility and high-flown sentiments; but there was something worse than 'to support the loss of the dearest friends and best society, and bear in exchange the tyranny, the exigence, the ennui and attempted indignities' of the Schwellenberg.

Miss Burney's heart had been touched by the singular attentiveness of the Queen's Vice-Chamberlain, who had the most seductive manners and, though a perfect gentleman, came constantly to her room of an evening, to the risk of her character. But he made no proposal of marriage, though a widower, soliciting her sympathies. Indeed, he was trifling with her affections; Miss Burney was moved to an outburst of indignation when she learned that he was to marry someone else. 'He has risked my whole earthly peace, with a defiance of all mental integrity the most extraordinary to be imagined! He has committed a breach of all moral ties with every semblance of every virtue.' In the published version of the Diary this is omitted, and he is given the name of Major Price. Actually he was a Colonel Digby, and evidently did not think Dr Burney's daughter, who was so sympathetic, quite good enough for him.

In 1788 Mrs Delany died, and the King went off his head. There has been a good deal of recent discussion whether there was not some hereditary taint in the stock; but anyone who knows what the poor King had to put up with for years, from both the politicians and his own sons, can hardly be surprised at his breakdown. He had begun his career exceptionally sheltered from the facts of life and with an abnormal lack of confidence in himself; when he discovered what people were really like, he found that he could manage very well for himself, but this involved an over-exertion of the will. Then there was the American war on his hands, which turned into a war against half the world; while driving Lord North on was a full-time job in itself. His sons were no help, they merely added to his headaches. The wonder is that he didn't break down before. At Windsor there was a great deal of coming and going; the Schwellenberg enjoined strict silence, but Queen Charlotte handed her husband over to the tender care of the Willises, who hustled him off to Kew and put him in a strait-jacket.

The King's recovery was greeted with joy, if not in Paradise, at any rate at Windsor. The town was ecstatic at his return – the doctors had had great difficulty in getting him away to the privacy of Kew; there were loyal addresses, bell-ringing, fireworks. Nor was it only the consideration of trade, the Castle's custom in the shops – though, many years afterwards, a Windsor boy remembered him as a quiet, courteous old gentleman turning over the books in the bookshops, or greeting the youngsters in the Park as he returned early in the morning from his dairy, of which he had made a success. 'Farmer George'; that is how people there saw him, and came to love him for his simplicity and courtesy, and the courage with which he came through the indignities of the treatment to which he was subjected.

The King expressed himself with his usual modesty in returning to his job in March 1789: 'though it might seem odd to mention one's health in a mere matter of business, I know how much Lord Sydney interests himself in my welfare that I just mention that the being returned to my favourite residence has obtained me a much quieter night than I had experienced since my illness; and the joy that appears in every countenance and the good sense of my neighbours in not wishing to incommode cannot fail of having a due effect.' There followed the inevitable routine: 'the body of people called Quakers' wanted to present a loyal Address; so did the now-loyal university of Oxford, so long distracted by Jacobite leanings.

Mr Powney had been appointed Ranger of Windsor Forest, but was then to fight an election for the borough; he now wants the Rangership for life, otherwise he would be 'unequal to the probable expenses of the election'. George III, recovered, knew two to that one: he was not convinced, 'from having too often found offices for life a ground of not supporting Administration'. Otherwise, 'I am well inclined to the late members for Windsor being re-chosen.' The Duke of Gloucester was made Keeper of Windsor Park and Forest, the Duke of Kent Ranger of the Home Park at Hampton Court: princelings must be provided for. Earl Howe actually asked the King for the governorship of the Castle – this was rather thrusting of him, but he was an aggressive sailor-type. Lord Euston wanted it too. The King gave it to neither, but appointed the Earl of Cardigan: he had long served the Crown, and 'attachment and fidelity should be reasonably rewarded'.

The old cart-horse was back in harness. Not well informed as to the acute political struggle that had raged around the Queen over the question of a regency, and the ill behaviour of her eldest son lining up with Charles Fox and the Opposition, Miss Burney luxuriated in tears. 'What a pleasure was mine this morning! how solemn, but how grateful! The Queen gave me the "Prayer of Thanksgiving" upon the King's recovery. It kept me in tears all the morning – that such a moment should actually arrive! after fears so dreadful, scenes so terrible.' This is what it was to be so sensitive – the Schwellenberg was made of sterner stuff. Her favourite amusement was watching her pet frogs eat the flies. Miss Burney handed the Prayer to dear Mr Smelt, a more sentimental German,

An engraving by C. Turner after a painting by R. B. Davis of
George III approaching Windsor, 1806.

'who took it from me in speechless ecstasy, his fine and feeling eyes swimming
in tears of joy'.

Mrs Schwellenberg wanted to take the air in the sharp frost; when others
beside Miss Burney were reluctant to enter the carriage, it was, 'O, ver well!
when they will serve me so, they might see what will become! No! it is not
permit!' etc. The old creature had a weakness for Queen Charlotte's wayward
sons. When the sailor Duke of Clarence, to become William IV, got tight at a
ball, it was, 'Vell! bin you much amused? Dat Prince Villiam – oders de Duke de
Clarence – bin raelly ver merry – oders vat you call tipsy.' Miss Burney was not
amused. When she resolved to give up her post, the dragon was furious, and
even more astonished at anyone daring to leave royal service. Miss Burney

pleaded her health, after five years of it: she could not explain to Queen Char-lotte that it was the perpetual presence of her faithful retainer that was 'subversive of my health, because incompatible with my peace, my ease, my freedom, my spirits, and my affections'.

Her retirement, after only five years of gilded servitude, did not commend her to Queen Charlotte, who, however, awarded her a modest pension of £100 a year, which gave her some independence. She was able to resume her far more interesting acquaintance with literary London, with Gibbon and Burke and Beckford, and even her former friend Mrs Thrale, whom everyone disapproved of for marrying her Italian musician, Piozzi. 'Who was that painted Foreigner?' Queen Charlotte had inquired on catching sight of her in St George's Chapel. That not all was loss to the writer in her Windsor experience we may judge from her novel *Camilla*, in which a lovely girl's affections are trifled with, and then is jilted by her beau for someone else. It was supposed to be the story of Mrs Delany's niece and companion at Windsor; however, might not something of the gallant (and errant) Colonel Digby had entered into it? Herself was now in a position to marry an impecunious French *émigré*. Since he was a count, and she now the Comtesse d'Arblay, she received from the Princesses, what they had not seen fit to confer before, an open invitation to the royal palaces.

George III returned with his usual appetite to his usual avocations. He was so fond of Windsor that often, when he had some boring job to perform in Lon-don, a levée at St James's, for example, he would ride up to town and back the same evening. Since he was so much there, a good deal of his Windsor corres-pondence is necessarily political. We must omit all that for what is personal and concerns the place. At some point he expressed his affection by inventing the Windsor uniform, 'blue and gold turned up with red'. A bit of a martinet, he had an eagle eye for detail. When there was a dispute between the Lord Steward and the Lord Chamberlain as to the right to the boxes under the gallery in St George's Hall, it was referred to the King, who knew it was the Lord Chamber-lain's. In that like his granddaughter Queen Victoria, who had a retentive memory for precedents – the great Lord Salisbury used to say 'we must ask the Queen'.

Most of the time life was very domestic, the evenings passed at Queen's Lodge, the daughters grouped round a large table with their work, books, pencils, paper. In the next room usually music from 8 to 10 p.m., chosen by the King, generally Handel, the family composer. On summer evenings King and Queen, arm in arm and followed by their dutiful girls, would walk up and down the Terrace greeting in friendly fashion their neighbours and all the folk who had come to see them. The crowd was so great that people pressed back against the wall to make way. The custom became a ritual.

We have a description of it from Dr Burney in 1799, as well as from his daughter earlier.

All was cheerfulness, gaiety and good humour, such as the subjects of no other monarch, I believe, on earth enjoy at present. I never saw it [the Terrace] more crowded or gay. The Park was almost full of happy people – farmers, servants and tradespeople – all in Elysium. Deer in the distance and *dears* unnumbered near. When the King and Queen, arm in arm, were approaching the place where the Herschel family and I had planted ourselves . . . the Queen said to his Majesty: 'There's Dr Burney,' when they instantly came to me, so smiling and gracious that I longed to throw myself at their feet.

"How do you do, Dr Burney?", said the King; "why, you are grown fat and young."

"Yes, indeed," said the Queen, "I was very glad to hear from Madame d'Arblay how well you looked."

After this the King and Queen hardly ever passed by me without a smile and a nod. The weather was charming; the Park as full as the Terrace, the King having given permission to the farmers, tradesmen and even livery servants during the time of his walking.

George III had a German conscientiousness about appointments, particularly clerical: he wanted to find the best men, and a respectable one if possible. This was unlike the English aristocratic standpoint expressed in the view that 'any English gentleman is qualified to hold any post he desires and considers proper to his station'. Once and again the King managed to balk the politicians of their prey, as when he forked John Moore, the Gloucestershire grazier's son, into the primacy, and so forestalled Charles James Fox (a Charles II descendant, who thought himself equal to any Hanoverian). On Moore's death the King repeated the manoeuvre. Pitt wanted the job for his Cambridge tutor, Pretty-man Tomline. But George III got in before him with an early morning visit to his Dean at Windsor, Manners-Sutton; the story is that all he said was, 'what a number of pairs of boots you have, your *Grace*'. It was enough.

Manners-Sutton's predecessor as Dean was Bishop Cornwallis. On his appointment his wife reports, 'the Bishop found his house at Windsor better than he expected, and his first residence there went off very well. I went with them to Court the day Miss Cornwallis was presented, but they are now so well acquainted with their royal neighbours that a Drawing-Room appears no longer formidable to them.' Here is a lady's view of things: her husband, already bishop of Lichfield, was doubling his job as dean of Windsor. Happy days! – for them.

Hanoverian Neglect; Georgian Domesticity

That respectability in morals was not a prerogative of George III we perceive from the Society for the Suppression of Vice, urged forward in 1806 by persons residing at Windsor. The public spectacle provided by his sons, all of them living in sin, gave some embarrassment to its secretary, who sought guidance from the Secretary of State. He felt 'embarrassed by scruples of respect and delicacy as to the propriety of extending its activity to the place of the King's residence and within the sphere of the example of the royal family'. This meddling person asked official advice as to 'the conduct most becoming in them to pursue on this occasion'.

For a change we have a vivid record of artistic personalities and happenings from the invaluable Farington Diary. Beechey was engaged in painting a rude

George III and his numerous children on the Terrace at Windsor.
'They would walk up and down the Terrace greeting in friendly
fashion their neighbours and all the folk who had come to see them.'

German princeling, another Württemberg – one of Queen Charlotte's relations – who kept the painter waiting three days. When the sitting was fixed,
he wouldn't sit still; the King, with his usual considerateness, engaged him in
conversation to get him to look in the right direction. At the end he wouldn't
even look at the picture but said that he would send one painted by a German
artist. Beechey painted an enormous canvas of George III reviewing some
regiment, which pleased him so much that, in addition to a large payment, he
knighted him. Later on, before his last illness, the King attacked Beechey for
taking advantage of him and imposing commissions on him. It is possible that
he had: everybody took advantage of the royal family. The dentist sent in a
bill for a year's attendance, of £3,000! This was a bit much, even if it included
the whole household: he was paid £1,500.

Benjamin West also took advantage of his situation. For Queen Charlotte's
entertainment at Frogmore in 1810 West got his son to do the drawings and
charge £500, 'a price which astonished the royal family'. For years West had
been treated with high favour: it is hardly surprising that he lost ground to
Wyatt. Wyatt, however, proceeded to employ *his* son to paint ceilings, though
quite inexperienced. The royal family were a milch-cow for them all: one
must remember this when one hears stories about George III's parsimony, or
Elizabeth I's. They were merely not silly like the Stuarts.

George III took an equally conscientious interest in Academy affairs – it
really was the Royal Academy then. There were factions within it, and in
August 1803 he received the President and Secretary to talk over their troubles.
The King was 'apprehensive there might have been extremes on both sides' and
wished to restore harmony. The President told him that some of the nobility
consulted him professionally 'to enhance the value of their purchases'. 'The
King had doubts whether the English have any true love for the Art.' (Perhaps
this was rather a German view.)

The scholarly antiquarian, Samuel Lysons, Keeper of Records at the Tower,
was regularly received at Windsor, and the King took a personal interest in the
magnificent project of the *Magna Britannia* – sad, however, when Lysons told
him it would take ten years to complete: he said it would be too long for *him*
to look forward to. It appeared that, after his illness, he had corrected his former
staccato manner of speaking 'so long habitual to him, and now speaks equally
and regularly without those repetitions'. Lysons brings him before us as he was,
before his final illness: 'sitting before the fire with his slippers on and several
newspapers – *The Times, Morning Post* and *Herald* – laid on the table. The King
rose on his coming in and continued standing, which he always does when any
person is with him. The general rule of etiquette is to appear to follow his
Majesty's lead as to the subject and not to contradict him.'

In 1804 a grand re-arrangement of pictures in the royal palaces was decided on, the King wishing the old masters to be concentrated at Windsor. When West came to discuss Academy business, the King talked much about the improvements in the Castle and took him round several rooms to show him the alterations. 'While preparing to examine the papers he said, "I am obliged at last to have recourse to spectacles, which I have strove against as long as I could."' Both Farington and Lawrence were well pleased with the improve-ments, scarlet hangings in the royal apartments, Copley's portraits of three of the children, massy silver tables brought from Hanover, sconces and chandeliers. The King had plenty of other things on his mind : there was the constant trouble his sons gave him. Then there was the ghastly Caroline whom he himself had wished on his son, the Prince of Wales, for a wife – no-one could have foreseen that she would prove so unspeakable. At the time of the 'Delicate Investigation' into the propriety of her conduct, which was neither proper nor delicate, she wanted to come to Windsor and throw herself on the King, now going blind. When his favourite daughter, young Princess Amelia, died he sank into his last long melancholy depression, and his son reigned in his stead as Regent.

During these ten years George III was confined at Windsor; his condition varied, sometimes he was able to strum on the key-board, sometimes he would look down on the Terrace and acknowledge the salute of the sentry below. There is a curiously attested story that, after his death, the sentries would see his white-bearded figure at the window raising his hand in salute. His death was the cue for a satire of wicked brilliance by Byron, *The Vision of Judgment*. It traverses, or rather travesties, George III's reign from a Liberal point of view. Liberals like Hazlitt or Lord Holland made heroes of Napoleon – though he knew how to deal with Liberals very well in his own country. Byron knew better than this, and in deploring 'the crowning carnage, Waterloo', wrote:

> Here Satan's sole good work deserves insertion –
> 'Tis that he has both generals in reversion.

The subject is the discussion at the celestial gate whether to receive the King:

> A better farmer ne'er brushed dew from lawn,
>   A worse king never left a realm undone!

Here is the regular Liberal cant, with George III made personally responsible for the wars of his time:

> He ever warred with freedom and the free:
>   Nations as men, home subjects, foreign foes,
> So that they uttered the word Liberty
>   Found George the Third their first opponent. Whose

George III. During his last ten years he was confined at Windsor in
his 'last long melancholy depression'.

Hanoverian Neglect; Georgian Domesticity

> History was ever stained as his will be
>   With national and individual woes?

Since the poet appeals to history, the historian may answer that history shows far worse records. The monarch is given credit for only the domestic virtues:

> I grant his household abstinence; I grant
> His neutral virtues, which most monarchs want;
> I know he was a constant consort, own
>   He was a decent sire, and middling lord.

But the poet is very rude about Queen Charlotte, and her son, the Regent:

> In whom his qualities are reigning still,
> Except that household virtue, most uncommon,
> Of constancy to a bad, ugly woman.

While the debate continues George III slips into heaven,

> And when the tumult dwindled to a calm,
> I left him practising the hundredth psalm.

Sir Jeffry Wyatville the architect who reconstructed the Castle for George IV.

6
George IV and Wyatville

ARCHITECTURE, to the informed eye, is history made visible. Just as Charles II's work at Windsor expressed the Restoration monarchy, its baroque splendour and cosmopolitan flavour, so George IV's re-fashioning of the Castle expressed the pride of Waterloo, the sense of triumph after twenty years' struggle with Revolutionary France and Napoleon, the emergence from it as the first nation in Europe, indeed at that time in the world. The consciousness of this is evident not only in Trafalgar Square or Waterloo Station, but in the cult of Waterloo, which received its expression in the great Chamber designed by Wyatville – and even, in a practical way, by the willingness of Parliament to grant an initial £150,000 for work on the Castle, knowing quite well that more would be needed. In the end £1 million was spent – and never did the nation get better value for its money.

All that was owing to George IV. When he died the Princess de Lieven wrote nostalgically of the days of his 'glory'. George IV certainly had a sense of glory – a rather rare quality in England: more common in France, where its exemplar was to be found, Louis XIV. George IV gave expression to it with his coronation, the grandest on record, his triumphal receptions in Scotland and Ireland (he even visited Hanover). There was in this an unspoken response to the age, a sense of triumph, after what efforts and sufferings, the relaxation and enjoyment of the Regency.

There went with this great taste, a response to the opulent and rich as well as to the elegant, a passion for objects of beauty that bordered on fantasy – and achieved such Coleridgean results with the pleasure-domes of the Pavilion at Brighton, with its Oriental inspiration, its Indian motifs and Chinese *décor*. The Regent had a life-long passion for French furniture and decoration, the finest in Europe. And this, though himself insatiable, he was almost able to satisfy. The Revolution threw on the market the most admirable works of art and craft, of cabinet-making and *ébénistes*, which the English aristocracy were able then to snap up. For the Revolutionary *canaille* emptied the palaces of their wonderful contents, and not only the royal palaces, Louvre and Tuileries, Versailles, St Cloud, Fontainebleau. Such people hate objects of beauty, which bring home to them their perennial inferiority, their essential meanness and envy. It had been the same with the incomparable collections of Charles I, which the Puritan Philistines of the Commonwealth dispersed.

George IV was perfectly aware of this, and even as Prince of Wales saw that he had an historic role to perform: 'we have lost the magnificent collection of Charles I; I will do what I can to supply its place'. Years later, when he had done what he could, he said of his own collection, 'I have not formed it for my own pleasure alone, but to gratify [*sc.* enlighten] the public taste, and lay before the artist the best specimens for his study.' No sovereign, except Charles I, was a more enlightened patron of the arts: Sir Thomas Lawrence, Hoppner, Wilkie; Nash, Soane, Wyatville; Chantrey, Westmacott; Sir Walter Scott; and in each of his residences there was a set of Jane Austen's novels – of how many monarchs later could that have been said?

Even in his own more cultivated age his passion for things of beauty was not appreciated for its true worth. People attributed his friendship with the Hertfords to his feeling for Lady Hertford – and it is true that he was sentimental, more than anything else, about women. But the real bond with the Hertfords was that strongest of bonds, with aesthetes, the passion for collecting: Lord Hertford was also a man of exquisite taste and made many purchases of furniture for the Regent in Paris. People were mistrustful of the influence of Sir Charles Long, who had been an acquaintance of George III and was a Tory; but he was a connoisseur, formed a collection of paintings and sculpture and advised both father and son on the decoration of the palaces. He also suggested valuable improvements for the streets and in the buildings of London; he urged the purchase of the Elgin Marbles, and was a first trustee of the National Gallery, which George IV was anxious to bring into being. He had given his father's splendid library to enrich the British Museum; he held two exhibitions of his own collection of paintings to instruct and enhance the public taste.

The plain fact, little realised, is that both George III and George IV were men of taste, and the son inherited it from the father. The history text-books fail to give them any credit for this; but then few historians, even a Macaulay, have much aesthetic or visual sense, concentrating as they do on the antics of politicians, that ephemeral ballet-dance of bloodless categories.

When George IV became king, at last, in 1820 he felt free to accomplish something worthy of the country, the age, and himself in his reconstruction of Windsor, which has been described, by an authority, as the greatest work of architectural improvement of the whole century. He also made it a treasure-house of the nation, in its splendid interiors, the furniture and paintings, the gold and silver plate, the priceless *objets d'art*. Though Wyatville was the architect, who did the stonework, George IV was the creator, who looked to everything else.

Right: The grand reception room.

Though derided by the fighting Philistines, who thought him unmartial, and treated badly by the politicians, who thought him wanting in courage, who accomplished the greater and more lasting achievement?

The Prince's earlier associations with Windsor were not happy: like most of the Hanoverian family, he did not get on with his father, and his mother was even more unsympathetic. Actually the youth was cleverer and more gifted – quite handsome when young – far more imaginative and with a romantic streak (responsive to the age bordering on fantasy), engaging and versatile, an amusing conversationist with a dangerous talent for mimicry, talkative, sentimental and indiscreet – made for trouble. He proceeded to give his overburdened father frightful trouble, for he was wildly extravagant and led astray by the aristocratic irresponsibles, the fashionables like Charles James Fox and Georgiana, Duchess of Devonshire, who gambled whole fortunes away. They were sworn enemies of the respectable King – no wonder he hated the idea of Charles Fox at the Treasury – and they took their revenge by leading his son astray. (They took a more lasting revenge through their epigoni, the Whig historians.)

The Prince quite early got into appalling debt (like the rest of them) and involved himself with undesirable (at any rate, in one sense of the word) women, like Perdita Robinson. It is thought that George III's first breakdown in 1788 had something to do with these worries. One day at Windsor the King had collared his erring son and shoved him up against the wall – a sound thrashing might have done no harm. Fox used the Prince as a catspaw to get back into power by agitating for a Regency, but the King's recovery defeated him.

At the concert given at the Castle to celebrate this happy event, the Prince and his favourite brother, the Duke of York, properly attended. The King was polite; Queen Charlotte, however, was 'sour and glum', and virtually told them that they were not wanted. And indeed it was turned into a Tory occasion: the ladies wore Tory colours, the confections decorated with loyal Tory slogans. Treated as an outcast, the Prince left in a huff. When he came down during the next year or two he would dine at the White Hart, spend the night in his apartments and depart without seeing his parents.

There was a reconciliation for the King's birthday ball, 4 June 1791, and never had 'Prinny' made a more splendid appearance: 'a bottle-green and claret-coloured striped silk coat and breeches, a silver tissue waistcoat, very richly embroidered in silver and stones and coloured silks in curious devices and bouquets of flowers'. Coat and breeches were covered with spangles; diamond buttons, epaulette and sword completed the outfit. For his own birthday ball on 12 August the reconciliation within the family – since the quarrels were equally public property – 'contributed in no small degree to add to the pleasures and festivities of the day'.

In 1795 he consented to marry, do his duty and beget an heir, in return for a financial settlement. He did not much care who his wife was to be – his heart was already elsewhere; it was bound to be some all too available German cousin. But this inattentiveness was a mistake, for Caroline of Brunswick, his first cousin, turned out to be unbearable, especially for a man of taste: for one thing, she didn't wash. On his wedding-night he was, understandably, drunk. His father did his best, as usual, and appeared on the Terrace escorting his daughter-in-law with 'entire gratification' – after all, she was his sister Augusta's daughter. The gratification soon lessened, for no-one could bear Caroline long; having given her the necessary child, the Prince ceased to live with her. Later on, there was a further quarrel over the child's bringing up, for he did not want the little Charlotte reared by her mother. Someone reported seeing the Prince at Windsor with his parents, out of spirits, out of humour with his mixed-up family life – and no wonder.

Himself fascinating, agreeable and kindly, he surrounded himself with more congenial companions. When, as Regent, he had to take over his father's responsibilities he came to appreciate the old King's difficulties; already, upon Charles Fox's death, he had declared that henceforth he would be no party-man. He was no fool, even about politics: in fact, he was a clever man, with his own devious ways of dealing with twisters. But he preferred the company of people who treated him sympathetically, or with deference, or with honesty – not all could combine all these qualities. The Conynghams, for example, were perfect gold-diggers; even these, however, made useful servants. The Regent's relations with Lady Conyngham were more sentimental than physical: he wanted domesticity, and this she gave him. Actually, she was bored by her servitude, and naturally expected her reward, which was considerable. Her husband was made a marquis in 1816; when George became king, the Marquis was made Constable of Windsor Castle and Lord Steward of the Household – the Conynghams constituted his household.

Nor were they always wrong – though the politicians fumed against the influence of 'the Lady'. When the Lady recommended her son's tutor for a vacant canonry at Windsor and the King appointed him, Lord Liverpool – who was a narrow-minded, middle-class type, very conscious of his dignity – was outraged. He made a Cabinet issue of the matter, he threatened to resign, he created a mountain out of a molehill. After this there was not much love lost between the King and his Prime Minister. Lord Liverpool, however, affronted him again by abetting the Dean and Chapter in their claim to walk on the

Terrace as and when they liked. The King said he would have maids and children staring in at his windows all day; for good measure, he described the Dean and Chapter as 'a more offensive and troublesome set of individuals to the King personally it is impossible to imagine'. Lord Liverpool never came down to Windsor more than he could help: someone passing him on the road down said that he must be going to administer a *stomacher*.

Lady Conyngham's recommendation to the canonry could not have been more suitable: Charles Richard Sumner was not only handsome and gentlemanly, a Tory, but decidedly religious, even an evangelical. George IV so took to him that he made him his librarian and private chaplain, with an extra £300 a year and 'a capital house opposite the Park gates'. When the fattest see, Winchester, became vacant the King forked him into it before the politicians could get after it: he was determined that his prelate of the Order of the Garter should be a gentleman. Sumner proved not only most munificent in his rich see, but positively reforming. But George IV, who experienced so many deceptions in life, was disappointed in the end. The Bishop, who had been a safe Protestant, scented which way the wind was blowing and went over to Catholic Emancipation in 1829. George's Protestant conscience could not forgive this, and another prelate was summoned to attend his death-bed.

Fortified by the prospect of a Parliamentary grant, George IV made a triumphal entry into Windsor on horseback in 1823. Next year he took up residence for a couple of months to consider what should be done, and on his birthday laid the foundation stone of the George IV Gate from the Park into the upper ward – a royal state-entrance. For the purpose a clearance was made of the Queen's Lodge: the Long Walk would have its logical termination at last. Parliament moved with alacrity 'for a degree of splendour that was becoming the sovereign who ruled over the country and also the country over which he ruled'. The grant was increased: the Princess de Lieven reported that 'the King is perfectly delighted that his Parliament has allowed him £300,000 for the restoration of Windsor Castle. It has put him in a good temper with his Ministers. English finances are magnificent. There has not been such internal prosperity for thirty years.'

Alas, all that was 150 years ago.

George IV had found his architect, and he was the right man for the job: Jeffry Wyatt, nephew of George III's architect, James Wyatt. At the stone-laying of his Gate the King had allowed him to change his name to Wyatville, to distinguish him from all the other Wyatts, and to bear a coat-of-arms with the simple motto, 'Windsor'. It proved a good omen, for all the scepticism of the wits:

Caroline of Brunswick, wife of George IV, who 'turned out to be unbearable, especially for a man of taste'.

A water colour by
Paul Sandby.

Above and Right: Illustrations of the alterations made by Sir Jeffry Wyatville, showing the structures after and before the changes were made.

> Let George, whose restlessness leaves nothing quiet,
> Change if He must the good old name of Wyatt;
> But let us hope that their united skill
> Will not make Windsor Castle Wyatt Ville.

In fact their skills were singularly united: never was there more harmonious cooperation between patron and architect – a marked contrast with the last monument to the nation's glory, Blenheim Palace, and the relations between Duchess Sarah and Vanbrugh. The King gave Wyatville the Winchester Tower to live in and to tether him to the spot. But Wyatville was conscientious and reliable and did not need watching, unlike his uncle and John Nash. This Midlander, with his extraordinary Midlands accent, became a much respected

member of the social scene – even more so with William IV, who enjoyed his company and would ask him to dinner almost every night.

Before that day there was an immense amount of work to be done – for which George IV showed his appreciation by knighting him when it was approaching completion, in 1828. During those four years there was a gigantic upheaval, for the surface of the upper ward was lowered three or four feet to give the buildings finer proportions; the earth was used to fill up the ditches and raise terraces. For four years some 700 men laboured on the works, with another seventy in London employed in preparing stone and lead and wood-work. The King was mostly in residence at the Cottage, or Royal Lodge, which he was also adding to and making most charming and agreeable. This was a large *cottage orné*, with thatched roofs. Conventional Queen Adelaide pulled most of it down, perhaps thinking it had been the scene of nameless orgies – more likely only bottomless sentimentalities.

Windsor Castle

This is not an architectural guide, and we can only summarise the main elements of the united achievement of king and architect. In the first place, and overwhelmingly, they integrated the Castle, gave the sprawling mass of buildings from various ages an artistic unity. This was the overriding aesthetic conception, which accounts even for its least pleasing feature, the texture of the stonework with the dark jointing in cement, accentuated by the use of flints. We in our day do not like it, but it was intended to bind the vast buildings together and elide the variations in the stonework of different periods.

On the other hand, anyone who compares the façades which Wyatville left with their appearance before will see how successfully he added to their interest and variety. He raised the buildings by a storey to accommodate servants, he heightened the towers and added others to accentuate the 'picturesque', a favourite note of the age, in which he had found the upper ward somewhat wanting. The result was a roofscape the fantasy of which everyone can appreciate, while his raising of the Round Tower by thirty feet was a stroke of genius, which gives a focal point to the whole.

The King's Cottage or Royal Lodge used frequently
by George IV as his residence.

He was an expert in achieving a rational plan of circulation within great houses – he had worked at Longleat and Chatsworth, and had been strongly backed by the Duke of Devonshire. Within the Castle he achieved this by the obvious measure of adding an external corridor to link up the three fronts around the upper ward; but he made a grander feature of it by making it of two storeys. It provided splendid vistas, if not so grand as those of the *Grand Monarque* at Versailles, but, when filled with the spoils of the Continent, conquering even Wellington or a grumpy Whig like Greville: 'magnificent and comfortable, the Corridor really delightful – furnished through its whole length of about 500 feet with the luxury of a drawing-room, and full of fine busts and bronzes, and entertaining pictures, portraits, and curious antiquities'.

To achieve a complete system of circulation within the buildings Wyatville had to demolish Hugh May's baroque chapel and St George's Hall. These were the saddest artistic losses, but were perhaps unavoidable. Wyatville did not wish to destroy the painted ceilings but he found that the state of the timbers rendered this necessary; in fact the extent of the rottenness and decay very much added to the expense of the work. He threw hall and chapel into a vast new St George's Hall of a Gothic character; if grandiose, grandeur was the intention. He provided a new main staircase to the state-apartments, later altered by Salvin; and he roofed over an ancient Brick Court to contrive the Waterloo Chamber, shrine of the cult, which George IV had the brilliant idea of decorating with the historic notabilities of the age that achieved victory over Napoleon, portrayed by its leading portrait-painter, Sir Thomas Lawrence.

Whatever fun might be made of Wyatville he and his patron brought off a splendid triumph. There was a chorus of contemporary praise, even from George IV's opponents: they could not resist his achievement when they saw it finished. He moved into it in 1828, when he had only two more years of life to enjoy it. The architect had wisely left the interior to the King's opulent taste, appropriate to a palace. The sense of space was increased by mirrors everywhere, and pierced or traceried doorcases. Cornices were enriched and gilded – Wyatville's own taste was simpler and more provincial; the superb doors and ebony bookcases were brought from Carlton House. At the same time work went on in the Park; besides that at the Cottage there was a Chinese pavilion on Virginia Water. Wyatville largely made Fort Belvedere, the little rococo castle on Shrub Hill, adding turrets and octagonal dining-room, with the Duke of Cumberland's cannon on the terrace – to have unhappy memories in our own squalid age.

By this time George IV had had quite enough of society and become a recluse at Windsor. His health was failing, but he roused himself for a last public appearance on his last birthday, in 1829, to lay the foundation of the vast statue

of George III to terminate the Long Walk on the horizon.

In the completed work, turreted and pinnacled and Gothic, we see in stone the Romantic conception of the age which the works of Walter Scott propagated in all the literatures of Europe.

Oddly enough Scott was less appreciative of the Castle than one might have expected – perhaps that was the eighteenth century side in him. He preferred the Cottage, where he stayed in 1826. 'His Majesty received me with the same mixture of kindness and courtesy which has always distinguished his conduct towards me. The King made me sit beside him and talk a great deal – *too much* perhaps, for he has the art of raising one's spirits, and making you forget the *retenue* which is prudent everywhere, especially at Court.' The Author of *Waverley* declared him every inch – he might have said, every ounce – a king. Next morning Sir Walter was taken to see the improvements at the Castle under Wyatville, of whom he says coolly, he 'appears to possess a great deal of taste and feeling for Gothic architecture. The old apartments, splendid enough in extent and proportion, are paltry in finishing.' Sir Walter wanted to see them all 'lined with heart of oak', like Abbotsford. George IV's taste was better.

Here was the background to the comings and goings of the notabilities of the age, foreign and homegrown, the politicians and clerics and – more congenial to the first inhabitant – artists and great ladies; to the politicising and gossip, the odd events and crises that filled the last years of the Castle's owner and re-creator.

One of the odder events concerned the curiosity about tombs, coffins and their contents which was a note of the age. During repairs in St George's Chapel in 1813 a workman spied three coffins in the vault of Henry VIII and Jane Seymour. Could the third be that of Charles I, about which there was some mystery, the exact spot of his burial having been forgotten?

On April Fool's day the coffin was opened in the presence of the Regent, curious as always, his brother Cumberland, the Dean of Windsor and Sir Henry Halford, the Court-doctor who amassed a fortune and was correspondingly unpopular. He published an account of what they saw:

the pointed beard was perfect ... the head was found to be loose and without any difficulty was taken up and held to view ... The hair was thick at the back ... and nearly black. A portion of it, which has since been cleaned is of a beautiful dark brown colour. That of the beard was of a redder brown ... The fourth cervical vertebra was found to be cut through its substance transversely, leaving the surfaces of the divided portions perfectly smooth and even, an appearance which could have been produced only by a heavy blow, inflicted with a very sharp instrument.

Halford, not content with reporting what they saw, abstracted the fourth

Left: The grand staircase as altered by Salvin.

cervical vertebra to show as a curiosity at his dinner-table. One or two other pieces were taken away too; it was not until late in Queen Victoria's reign that they were restored to their owner – or at least his coffin, in the presence of another Prince of Wales. Byron could not let this event pass without a lash at the Regent:

> Famed for contemptuous breach of sacred ties,

– what about himself? –

> By headless Charles see heartless Henry lies;
> Between them stands another sceptred thing –
> It moves, it reigns – in all but name a king.
> Charles to his people, Henry to his wife –

– what about himself? –

> In him the double tyrant starts to life:
> Justice and Death have mixed their dust in vain,
> Each royal Vampire wakes to life again.
> Ah, what can tombs avail, since these disgorge
> The blood and dust of both to mould a George!

No historian, Byron evidently thought that George was descended from both Henry VIII and Charles I: he was descended from neither.

An even more macabre event in its way was the funeral of George IV's brother, the Duke of York, on the bitterly cold night of 20 January 1827, which led to the death of several of the eminent elderly who attended it. George IV had sent Knighton, teeth chattering and by the light of a solitary torch, down into the royal vault to select a resting-place as near as possible to George III on the ground that Frederick was his father's favourite. On the night of the funeral the Cabinet dined with Canon Long, Sir Charles's brother, who had thus been provided for. Lord Westmorland characteristically lost himself in the Cloisters, thought he was dining with Sir Charles, and had left his collar of the Garter behind him.

After dinner they were summoned by the heralds to the Chapel, all were marshalled, royal dukes and everybody. But the coffin didn't arrive for two mortal hours; the night was freezing, the paving stones damp, there was no matting. The elderly gentlemen began to suffer: Mr Canning persuaded old Lord Chancellor Eldon to stand on his cocked hat, but himself caught a chill from which he never recovered, and Huskisson fell seriously ill. When the coffin arrived between the flickering torches, the gear for lowering it into the vault failed and it had to be left above ground. The Cabinet returned to Canon Long's to divest themselves of their Orders; Wellington had worn three: the

Garter, the Bath, and the Golden Fleece. The last had been the Emperor Charles v's, given to the Iron Duke by the Emperor of Austria.

The Duke suffered no ill effects, but it was said that the ultimate toll of that night was two bishops, five footmen and several soldiers, not to mention the Cabinet ministers.

And so to the politicians.

George iv has been much underestimated as a political figure too, partly as the result of the irresponsible vagaries of his youth under Charles Fox's tuition, still more from the misrepresentations of the Whig intellectuals whose hopes he deceived. For, when he came to face the facts of political responsibility

Sandby R A pinx.   *M A Rooker sculp.*

THE NEW LODGE, *built by the late Duke of Cumberland, on* SHRUBS HILL. *WINDSOR FOREST.*

Fort Belvedere, 'the little rococo castle on Shrub Hill'.

he became, to them, an apostate. He was cleverer and more devious than his father – a necessary quality in a politician; and he had quite different techniques – a whole battery of charm and loquacity: interviews with him might last two or three hours, two recorded interviews in the political crises of 1827 lasted five hours, in which the King talked most of the time; to this were added at will sighs, tears, protestations of affection, embraces, kisses. He usually managed to get his way – after all he was the king-pin.

Even Wellington – very much a no-nonsense man, who came up against him over several critical issues – could not help admiring him: 'the most extra-ordinary compound of talent, wit, buffoonery, obstinacy and good feeling – in short a medley of the most opposite qualities, with a great preponderance of good – that I ever saw in any character in my life'. He was on any reckoning, and in both senses of the word, an outsize man. ('Prinny has let his belly down; it reaches to his knees', reported Creevey.) Perhaps the most notable thing about him was his vitality, the zest that carried him on. He was extremely well informed, and had an absolute passion for gossip – also useful in his job. People thought he was idle and indolent; but in his later years, when he was suffering from prostate trouble, he worked a great deal in bed, like Sir Winston Churchill. Greville, who was Clerk of the Council, found that the King got through his boxes and did much reading in bed; though by now a recluse, he knew every-thing that was happening. He would relieve the tedium of Council meetings by jokes, some of them good, like that about the Admiral who had demolished the Turkish fleet at Navarino by a happy misunderstanding: 'I have given him the Ribbon, but I should have given him the rope.'

Shortly after the fatal funeral at Windsor Lord Liverpool died, and there was an acute crisis as to who was to succeed him. Canning was popular enough in the country, but – a man of genius – he was distrusted by some of his colleagues, envied by others, and objected to by a number of aristocratic snobs, though they had been at Eton with him, because of his origins. (Left an impoverished widow, his mother had gone on the stage to support herself and her children – *any* other profession would have been preferable.) In the background loomed the issue of Catholic Emancipation – unpopular in England, but becoming the irresistible aim of national agitation in Ireland. Both parties, Tory and Whig, were splitting up; the political situation was most confused: the King had to make the choice.

There was much coming to and fro between London and Windsor. Though Tories, Wellington and Peel in the end would not serve under their colleague, Canning. They were unreasonable, but they were not the only politicians to be so. While the crisis continued Greville reports to us how things were at Windsor. The King was still at the Cottage: 'after waiting two hours and a

Above right: Wyatville's design for the royal dining-room.
Below right: Charles II's dining-room.

Overleaf: Queen Victoria entertains King Louis-Philippe at a grand banquet in St George's Hall.

half, ushered into his bedroom, I found him sitting at a round table near his bed, in a *douillette*' [dressing gown]. Later that month he was up and about, in health and spirits:

he had a large party at the Lodge last week, and Canning, the Granvilles, Carlisles, Lievens, are going there next week. Mount Charles [the Conynghams' son] told me that next week something must be decided . . . that the King's opinions on the Catholic question are just the same as those of the Duke of York, and equally strong. This is the great difficulty which Canning has to get over with him. Mount Charles told me that his mother has strong opinions in favour of the Catholics, but that she never talks to the King on the subject, nor indeed upon politics at all.

Here is one indication of George IV's independence of mind, for he was himself rootedly opposed to Catholic Emancipation. Here is another: the Iron Duke came down to Windsor and presented the King with a blunderbuss. He said he would not submit to dictation, and – quite as sensitive as his father as to his prerogative – he appointed Canning. He did not much like him, but he had made the right choice: Canning got together a middle-of-the-road government, against both extreme wings, and found a majority in Parliament. George IV had interpreted the will of the nation, as Queen Anne had done in calling on Harley against her own overmighty Duke.

In July the King wished to see Wellington at Windsor again. He received the Duke 'MOST graciously' and held him in conversation for two and a half hours. Wellington got the impression that the King wanted him back to strengthen Canning, and this was a good idea; for Canning was now ill, and in August he died. All was to do all over again. The political situation was in confusion; in Ireland the agitation for Catholic Emancipation grew. George held forth to one visiting peer that he had better take over the government himself: 'there was no man in England capable of giving him advice upon any subject whatever'. If this was rodomontade it was at any rate understandable. When he sought the Duke's advice upon foreign affairs in November, George took him for a tour all round the Levant: 'he then set off full gallop, took me from the seat of war into the Ionian Islands', and then all round Europe; 'at last after a discourse of at least an hour and a quarter he brought me home to Windsor Castle'.

There the works were still not finished; he needed another grant from Parliament: he had elicited the Duke's support. Greville had heard Wyatville lobbying Herries, one of the commissioners for the restoration, for money to finish the Round Tower. Herries said, 'will you do it for £10,000?' Wyatville said, 'you must give me £15,000'. From this exchange Greville inferred that Herries was to be Chancellor of the Exchequer, and this proved correct.

Left: The Waterloo Chamber hung with the famous Lawrence portraits.

Next year the King was in acute anxiety about a threatened suspension of the works – he had been spending prodigious sums on furniture, commissioning paintings, etc. – and wrote to Knighton about the danger of dispersing such an immense body of workmen, impossible to collect together again, and 'complete the whole with the *same degree* of *perfection* and *solidarity* with which the present existing part is done and which speaks for itself'. He did not wish to see Wyatville 'brought to this disgraceful and really abominable dilemma'.

He appealed to the Duke, now Prime Minister, who loyally supported him with a further grant and gave orders for the work to proceed with all speed. It was virtually completed this year; the King moved in, Wyatville's bust by Chantrey was placed in the Gate with which the work was begun, and his portrait painted by Lawrence – one of his best renderings of character. Wellington took the Arbuthnots down to see the work in its concluding stages and could not but be delighted with it. In the Waterloo Chamber Mrs Arbuthnot particularly admired the portraits of Pius VII and Consalvi. They all thought the new apartments quite beautiful and George IV's Gateway 'perfection'; the whole thing now, in the summer of 1828, was already 'magnificent'.

The nation had indeed got value, as rarely, for its money.

By now George IV was a sick man: he had a constant 'irritation in the bladder which he could not get rid of'. In the rooms in the Castle, where Queen Charlotte had so complained of the cold, her son achieved a hot-house atmosphere and kept out the air; people couldn't bear it and his attendants were driven to drink. He himself was forced to take laudanum to dull his pain and get some sleep. Greville reports that 'his Majesty keeps everybody at a great distance from him, and all about him are afraid of him, though he talks to his pages with more openness and familiarity than to anybody. He reads a great deal, and every morning has his boxes brought to him and reads the contents.' His strong vitality kept him going, and he could rouse himself on occasion. Greville says he kept the Council waiting an hour and then appeared 'in a blue great-coat all over gold frogs and embroidery . . . The King is the greatest master of gossip in the world, and his curiosity about everybody's affairs is insatiable.' Not unnaturally he knew everything about everybody, like Louis XV through the *Secret du Roi*.

In December 1828 he gave a reception at the Castle for the little Queen of Portugal, at which he appeared at his best. Everybody agreed that it was charming; the Princess de Lieven was entranced by his addressing the little girl alternately as 'your Majesty' and 'my dear'. He overwhelmed her with kindness, drinking her health as 'Queen and my ally'. No-one commented that he was perhaps making up a little for Canning's support of the independence of her

Right: The Round Tower as raised by Wyatville in 1828.

Ernest Augustus, Duke of Cumberland who encouraged George IV in his opposition to Catholic Emancipation.

colonies in South America. He was still adding to the Cottage for his summer residence, and entertaining a party of leading Whigs. In January he entertained the Lievens; he was ill and losing weight, but was 'most gracious, charming and attentive to everybody ... I hardly ever remember to have passed more pleasant days with him. The Castle is magnificent in the extreme: luxury can hardly be carried further, and comfort is equally well looked to.'

In this last year, Greville reports, 'he leads a most extraordinary life – never gets up till six in the afternoon. They come to him and open the window curtains at 6 or 7 a.m.; he breakfasts in bed, does whatever business he can be brought to transact in bed too, he reads every newspaper quite through, gets up in time for dinner, and goes to bed between ten and eleven. He sleeps very ill, and rings his bell forty times in the night; if he wants to know the hour, though a watch hangs close to him, he will have his *valet de chambre* down rather than turn his head to look at it.' But, in fact, he was going blind. At a Council held by candlelight he could not see to read the list, but Greville was 'so good a courtier that I held the candle in such a way as to enable him to read it himself'. He was as clever and amusing as ever, and had an extraordinary memory; but, what with the laudanum and all the potions he took, his fantasies grew upon him. One day he told the Duke that Lord Chesterfield, the mentor of decorum, had advised him as a young man: 'Stick to your father: as long as you adhere to your father you will be a great and a happy man. But if you separate yourself from him you will be nothing and an unhappy one.' George IV added blissfully, 'And, by God, I never forgot that advice, and acted upon it all my life.'

The Duke and the others who heard this declaration, and knew the record, looked at each other with astonishment. The wheel had come full circle: with a comparable experience of life and men George IV had come round to his father's point of view.

He had yet one more political struggle before him – over Catholic Emancipation. People do not seem to realise why he felt so strongly, just like his father, over this. It was at root a Hanoverian conviction. The House of Hanover had been awarded the throne precisely because they were Protestants. George III and George IV had a scruple of conscience about the senior line whose place they had taken: they were nothing if not Protestants. It was not only the question of their coronation oath, though that gave them pause too. For them giving way to Catholic claims raised a moral as well as a political problem – the validity, or at least the purity, of their own claim.

During the political crisis from which Canning's ministry emerged George IV had managed to impose terms and stave off the dreadful day. No fool at the game, he lobbied individual peers. When the Duke of Newcastle came down to Windsor, after waiting a couple of hours he was nearly asleep when the King came in and held forth for another hour on Catholic Emancipation. He repeated the whole history of the question from James II onwards, but for whose stupidity he would never have been there, and declared himself 'a Protestant, heart and soul'. He added that 'the courage of his family had never been questioned' (his own had): he would *never* assent. Next month, of a six hour interview with archbishops and bishops he talked for five hours. He saw to it that he got the Church behind him, he had the country at large, and he got his way.

But Ireland was becoming ungovernable without it; opinion was changing in England and we have seen that his own favourite bishop wobbled (Sumner repented later). The irony was that it fell to Wellington, of all people, to introduce the measure and force George IV's hand. The King, whom people mistakenly thought a coward because he was an aesthete, fought back, ill as he was. He reinforced his conscience by the support of the unpopular Cumberland, now that the popular York was no more; he tried to winkle away Tory votes and to make the Royal Household vote against the measure.

Wellington determined on a showdown and came down to Windsor. The King put up a five-hour battle – several of his hero's battles had hardly taken as long; every weapon was called into play, tears, expostulations, arguments, history, he wept for his Protestant conscience. In the end he assented to the Speech promising Catholic relief, and the Prime Minister was dismissed with a royal kiss and an arm round his neck. But when the Duke was out of the way George IV went back on what the Duke, used to simpler engagements, had taken for capitulation. Wellington was furious and went forward with the measure. It passed with an unexpected majority. The King talked of retiring to Hanover, where his family had come from. But it was too late, he was too tired and ill: 'the Royal Assent was extracted rather than given'.

On one of his last drives in the Park the Duchess of Kent with her little daughter Victoria met the King. The fabulous old creature, rouged and bewigged, invited the little girl, to her mother's trepidation, into the phaeton. 'Give me your little paw', the monster said. It seems to have been the only time that she set eyes on the monarch whose presumptive heiress she was.

When death came to him he confronted it bravely enough; he took the Sacrament – but not from the bishop who had deserted him over Catholic Emancipation. Next day, feeling better, he talked of going to Ascot; his chaplains did not think it necessary to administer the sacred elements again. At the funeral his successor, overwhelmed at his good luck, talked all through the service.

William IV's seven years at Windsor were something of a comic postscript to George IV's. Though William was more popular, he had nothing of his brother's achievements or prestige, and far less gumption. His accession almost turned his head at the beginning. When the Princess de Lieven went down to Windsor under the new régime she found people, especially middle-class people, remembered George IV only to criticise his morals. Of course they didn't know what he was really like, but 'what a nation most appreciates in its sovereign is domestic virtue'. With respectable Queen Adelaide at his side, the new king in his present manifestation provided this spectacle. But for many years he had lived with Mrs Jordan, the actress, by whom he had a numerous progeny who were now to be provided for.

The situation was not lost on Dorothea de Lieven: 'the day after the King's funeral he took possession of Windsor Castle, where the Ministers and great officers of the Household awaited him. He arrived perched outside a small carriage, in which were the Queen and his two bastard daughters.'

After the seclusion of his brother in the fantasy world he had created, William IV enjoyed showing himself to the mob, and the mob responded. He threw open all the private walks and drives in the Park, and even the Terrace, to the public; he replaced the bust of the Whig Duke of Bedford which George IV had banished from his gallery, and this pleased the Russells. On the whole he was prepared to do what the politicians told him, and this eased the way for Parliamentary Reform. Once he settled into his popular gait, with his head that looked remarkably like a pineapple, he took to ceremonial life in the Castle which he had never seen over before. He was prepared to put the finishing touches on his brother's work, though giving the instruction, 'No gilding.' He made even one useful addition: he carried out Lord Grey's suggestion of turning Elizabeth I's gallery into a Library.

Naturally affable and friendly he entertained hugely. On his first birthday as king he gave a banquet in St George's Hall; Greville describes it as 'the finest thing possible – all good and hot, and served on the late King's gold plate. There were one hundred people at table. After dinner the King gave the Duke of Wellington's health, as it was the anniversary of Vimeiro. I can't agree with Charles X that it would be better to '*travailler pour son pain* than to be King of England'. (That ass, another James II, ended up like him in exile.)

Greville has a wonderful description of the large party for Ascot, William IV asking each day a crowd from the neighbourhood. There were forty people at dinner; 'he drinks wine with everybody, asking seven or eight at a time. After dinner he drops asleep.' There was a band and instrumental music. The King took the party along to see the Hall and ball-room, 'where we walked about, with two or three servants carrying lamps to show the proportions. The whole thing is exceedingly magnificent.' Greville could not but note the contrast with the life of the artist-king who had refashioned it all.

The Castle holds very few people, and with the King's and Queen's immediate suite and *toute la bâtardise* it was quite full. The King's four sons were there, *signoreggianti tutti*, and the whole thing *donnait à penser* to those who looked back a little and had seen other days. We sat in that room in which Lyndhurst★ has often talked to me of the famous five hours' discussion with the late King, when the Catholic Bill hung upon his caprice . . . What a *changement de décoration*: no longer George IV capricious, luxurious, and misanthropic, liking nothing but the society of listeners and flatterers, with the Conyngham tribe and one or two Tory Ministers and foreign ambassadors; but a plain, vulgar, hospitable gentleman, opening his doors to all the world, with a numerous family and suite, a Whig Ministry, no foreigners, and no toad-eaters at all.

One thing was quite continuous with the Hanoverians – their family quarrels. Nobody liked the Duchess of Kent, mother of young Princess Victoria, now heiress to the throne. This German woman was utterly tactless, ill-humoured with everybody, except Sir John Conroy, her adviser who seems to have been excessively close to her. George IV, 'who was as great a despot as ever lived, was always talking of taking her child from her'. Partly because of this, she kept the girl in seclusion: few people, including leading figures like Palmerston, had ever seen her until she became queen.

Now the Duchess set herself in opposition to William IV, as kindly an old fellow as ever was and very well disposed to his niece. She started taking the little Princess round the country to be saluted by ships of the Navy and civic dignitaries, infuriating William who can hardly have wanted his demise anticipated. Then the Duchess, against his permission, appropriated to herself and her daughter a suite of seventeen rooms in Kensington Palace. This precipitated an outrageous public outburst by the sailor-King, before a hundred persons, at one of his last banquets at Windsor. The Duchess and her daughter were present when William openly attacked 'that person now near me, who is surrounded by evil advisers, and who is herself incompetent to act with pro-priety in the situation in which she would be placed. I have been insulted – grossly and continually insulted – by that person,' he went on. Then, pointing to the Princess, he complained of her being kept away from his Court, kept away from his Drawing-rooms at which it was her duty to appear as the heiress-presumptive. He went on and on, for, like his brother, he had a natural vein of eloquence – only George IV exercised his in private, William in public. Every-one was aghast; the Princess in tears – it was a rude introduction to the amenities of public life; after dinner the Duchess ordered her carriage.

The interesting thing is that secretly, unknown to anyone, the girl's sympa-thies were with the King, not with her mother – perhaps so strong are the unique

★ Lord Chancellor Lyndhurst was the son of the American painter John Singleton Copley.

204

affiliations of royal ties as against private ones. Though no-one had any idea 'what She is or what She promises to be', she already knew where her duty lay and a royal confidence in herself.

The elderly King had a good phrase when dying: 'this is the 18th of June: I should like to live to see the sun of Waterloo set'.

And the young girl, named for the victory, reigned in his stead.

Queen Victoria and Wellington reviewing troops.

7
The Victorian Age

SOMEONE has said that if Windsor reached its peak artistically with George IV, it achieved its apogee socially in Queen Victoria's reign. It was certainly then that it was made grandest and widest use of. And this in spite of the fact that she was not fond of it. Contrary to the popular conception of her, she much preferred the comparative informality of Balmoral and Osborne, which the Prince Consort and she built and created. In 1858 she is writing to her daughter Vicky – to become the German Empress Frederick: 'I have never felt Windsor more dull and tiresome – or the Castle stiffer and gloomier than this year! I long for our cheerful and unpalacelike rooms at Osborne and Balmoral.' At another time she calls it 'prison-like' – and this before the death of the Prince Consort there: that added to its sadness, but she turned it into his shrine, and that reconciled her.

For her it meant work and duty, the weary round, the authority of the state, the sense of her place in it and the dignity proper to it – as she laid down, quite early on, to Albert: 'I am the Sovereign.' Not that she objected to work, duty and the rest of it, but that, with her, Windsor took the place of the capital. Like her grandfather George III, and her uncle George IV (in his later years), she disliked London and made increasingly infrequent appearances there. Windsor was as near as she would come to living in London; everybody of importance came down to the Castle. And, sooner or later, everybody who had accomplished anything in the country or the Empire was invited there 'to dine and sleep'. She was very good about that – and this in addition to the hordes of her family wide-spread throughout Europe, the visiting royalties, the political leaders whom she had to see, the clerics and the bishops. Bishops she did not much care for: 'the Queen must honestly confess that She has never found people promoted to the Episcopate remain what they were before'.

All this meant that, though people grew to think of her as a recluse, this was not true: she saw everybody and knew most of what was going on. Apart from her preference for peace and quiet, which she could rarely get, there may have been some unconscious art in her withdrawal. When the American Duchess of Marlborough was invited with her husband 'to dine and sleep', the democratic eye of Consuelo Vanderbilt perceived that the assertion of royal dignity, the silence around the old lady, the build-up of ritual, the kissing of hands, all was deliberate and considered. Queen Victoria was a dinky little woman: withdrawal from the public gaze into being an hieratic symbol was a much more effective way of maintaining the dignity, and even the authority, of a sovereign – as it had been with Philip II, no large impressive figure but a small man, ruling half the world (as he wrote) from within the walls of the Escorial.

At the same time simple dignity was natural to her: everyone noticed this in the girl-Queen, after the undignified ways of William IV. At her first visit as queen she observed that the flag was still at half-mast: it would have been better to have given an order, in case anyone thought it necessary to elevate it on her arrival. Melbourne was surprised – he hadn't given it a thought, 'but it showed her knowledge of forms and her attention to trifles'. Thus Greville: 'With all her prudence and discretion she has great animal spirits, and enters into the magnificent novelties of her position with the zest and curiosity of a child.'

After the long rule of elderly gentlemen in various stages of invalidism it was something to have a girl of eighteen at the head of society. Byron's friend Hobhouse was at the Castle for a large party in September 1837, when she went for the first time to visit Virginia Water. She liked being accompanied by a large troupe on horseback; they all poured rapidly through the glades of the forest until they arrived at George IV's Chinese Pavilion. Hobhouse had

never looked at the scene before, and could fancy myself on the banks of some Swiss or Tyrolese lake. The Queen and her attendants got into the state barge, with the standard of England flying on it, and were rowed to the opposite bank ... The Royal party landed at the Pavilion, and the Queen ordered the frigate to be got under way. This pretty miniature man-of-war was manned by a lieutenant and six sailors. When opposite to the Pavilion the frigate began to salute, and fired her one-and-twenty guns with great precision. A very pretty effect was produced by the smoke, burnished by the setting sun, rolling away on the surface of the lake.

In these first years her Prime Minister, Lord Melbourne, was at her side, at table, after dinner in the evenings, riding in the Park, often for five hours a day. She adored him: to her he was the father-figure she had never had and was always in need of; on his side, he was tutoring her, teaching her chess, instructing her in politics and life, though never taking advantage of his exceptional position in a partisan way. He did not need to; for, with her one-track mind and force of temperament, she was a fierce Whig, irrationally prejudiced against all Tories, and could not abide the thought of a change of her Ministers. There was no room for half-shades with her. Everyone admired the propriety of Melbourne's conduct, and many were amused at the transformation wrought in this old Regency *roué*, dancing attendance on his Virgin Queen morning, noon and night, listening to her artless platitudes – he, who had been reared in the sophisticated conversation of Holland House – watching her riding in flowing habit down the line of redcoats at her first military review in the Great Park. If not precisely in love with the girl himself, it was at any rate a virginal romance, after the deceptions he had endured from more experienced women.

His fellow-Whig Greville has a rather acidulated portrait of the new régime. 'She sits at a large round table, her guests around it, and Melbourne always in a chair beside her, where two mortal hours are consumed in such conversation as can be found, which appears to be, and really is, very uphill work. His manner to her is perfect, always respectful, and never presuming upon the extra-ordinary distinction he enjoys. Hers to him is simple and natural, indicative of the confidence she reposes in him and of her lively taste for his society.' He must have been the most amusing man she had ever conversed with – herself with no conversation, for she had never met anybody much and had no general ideas. (She had been taught only languages, and was a good linguist, speaking German and French with fluency.) Greville thought it astonishing that Melbourne 'could endure the life he leads. Month after month he remains at the Castle, submitting to this daily routine. Never was such a revolution seen in anybody's occupations and habits. Instead of indolently sprawling in all the attitudes of luxurious ease, he is always sitting bolt upright. His free and easy language interlarded with "damns" is carefully guarded with the strictest propriety, and he has exchanged the good talk of Holland House for the trivial, laboured, and wearisome inanities of the Royal circle.'

The young Queen 'orders and regulates every detail herself, she knows where everybody is lodged in the Castle, settles about the riding or driving, and enters into every particular with minute attention'. Clever Mr Greville, Clerk of the Privy Council, could not bear it: sitting for hours of an evening playing shilling-whist with the Duchess of Kent was not his idea of bliss. And even some Court-ladies were driven to despair: one of them, asked where she was going, said 'out into the town'.

Palmerston, brought up in the ways of the Regency, could not acclimatise himself and tried to vary the amusements. 'Always enterprising and audacious with women, he took a fancy to Mrs Brande, and at Windsor Castle, when she was in waiting and he was a guest, he marched into her room one night. His tender temerity met with an invincible resistance. The Lady did not conceal the attempt and it came to the Queen's ears.' Victoria was outraged and regarded it as an insult to herself. Melbourne had the greatest difficulty in papering this

Overleaf: Queen Victoria riding in Windsor Park with Lord Melbourne.

over, 'abhorring an *esclandre* in which his colleague and brother-in-law would have so discreditably figured. Palmerston got out of the scrape with his usual good luck, but the Queen has never forgotten and will never forgive it.' We now know the real reason for her detestation of him: it was not just politics – and she had an extraordinarily tenacious memory.

What was needed was a husband for the young woman, a family to carry on the succession, a male head of the household, a man such as she always needed by her side. Uncle Leopold, King of the Belgians, was frequently at Windsor; he would have been there permanently if only his wife, Princess Charlotte, had not died in the attempt to provide an heir. As it was he enjoyed a pension from the British state, a milch-cow for them all. He was a Coburg, of that impecunious family which was to have such prodigious dynastic success in that century – sooner or later, everybody seemed to marry a Coburg. He had two available nephews, who were brought over for inspection in October 1839. Victoria fell in love with Albert at once; she took, as she said, only an hour to make up her mind. He was very good-looking; he knew his dynastic duty, and all the Coburgs knew which way their bread was buttered. He was not very responsive to women: there would be no trouble that way. Within a matter of days the betrothal was announced, Albert looking well in dark blue Windsor uniform with red facings. He addressed his bride to be as 'vortrefflichste', and – 'I shall never cease to be a true German.'

He was, in fact, a 'good German', and a great servant of the British state, though never popular in England. In Parliament Tories and Radicals combined to cut his allowance from the proposed £50,000 to £30,000. Uncle Leopold thought this 'intolerable'; but the English thought *him* grasping. Immediately after the wedding-breakfast, 10 February 1840, the couple drove down to Windsor for their honeymoon in shabby style in an old travelling coach, her friends lamenting 'at her not conforming more than she is doing to English customs'. Married on Monday, she collected an immense party for Wednesday; on Tuesday morning Greville said to Lady Palmerston that 'this was not the way to provide us with a Prince of Wales'. However, there were the stimulating enjoyments of having Albert put on her stockings and watching him shave. It was early made clear that 'everything is to bend to her will': he could only advise 'the Sovereign'.

From her wedding she had kept the Tories away as far as possible and Greville, though a Whig, was shocked at the difficulty Melbourne had had in prevailing upon her to invite Wellington to the Castle. 'It is very revolting to hear of a girl of nineteen, albeit Queen, pronouncing an opinion upon the conduct of the Duke of Wellington and deciding what it was his duty to do. She will have

Victoria and Albert at Windsor with the Princess Royal 1842.
Painting by Landseer.

to learn the disagreeable lesson that her opinion does not make right, nor her
volition law.' She changed her mind about Wellington, when she learned
better; but the trait remained the same: Albert confessed later that he was
always afraid of contradicting her, 'because of the hereditary taint in the
family'.

The best quality she had to carry her through was her extraordinarily strong
common sense – she too, like the Duke, was a 'no-nonsense' person and this
drew them together: she came to appreciate him at his true value. Then there
was her genuine kindness and warmth of heart: she was exceedingly kind to
the whole tribe of William IV's bastards, each of whom had got £30,000 out
of their father. One of them, Lord Munster, was Constable of the Castle,

another had the Rangership of the Park; when Lord Grey's Economical Reforms abolished the latter it was compensated to the tune of £4,000 a year.

Full of prejudice, she was yet never a snob – a prime qualification for success in a Royal personage. The mayor of Newport had done good service against the Chartists and been knighted, but thought 'etiquette would not permit one of his rank in life to be invited to the Royal table'. This was held to be nonsense: if he was good enough to be knighted he was good enough to dine there. He behaved himself much better than some aristocrats, or even than the late monarch, 'with complete self-possession and a *nil admirari* manner which had something distinguished in it. The Queen was very civil to him, and he was delighted.'

The eminent historian Guizot, who happened to be Louis Philippe's Prime Minister, did much less well: 'he committed a great *gaucherie*, which he never could have done if he had had more experience of Courts'. The first night at dinner he was placed next to the Queen; the second night when he was to sit next to the Queen of the Belgians he protested to the Lord Chamberlain, '*ma place est auprès de la Reine*'. The Queen quickly and wisely accommodated him. Nor did Macaulay make a much better figure, when a Council was held at the Castle to swear him in. He was too voluble and hostile to the Chinese, calling for war-measures; he talked too much as always. In September 1840 a Council was held to introduce Prince Albert; no-one occupied Melbourne's chair next to the Queen – it was left vacant like Banquo's till he should come back.

But a change of government was under way: nothing the little Queen could do would prevent it. Greville discovered the odd habit people had in the Castle of writing each other from room to room – it was partly that the Queen never liked a direct discussion face to face. She was making difficulties, objecting to Sir Robert Peel and so on. For Ascot there was a gorgeous banquet for a hundred people in St George's Hall, 'very magnificent, blazing with gold plate and light, and very tiresome'. The great French actress Rachel – we remember Arnold's sonnet about her – declaimed: Greville found it fatiguing, 'but it served to occupy the evening, which is always the great difficulty in Royal society. The Queen was pretty well received on the course, and her party consisted in great measure of Tory guests.' The new Ministers had been given a good reception by her; but Peel 'could not help putting himself into his accustomed attitude of a dancing-master giving a lesson. She would like him better if he would keep his legs still.' She herself thought that he had not much sense of character, and she was right; thus her own political education proceeded.

Prince Albert, however, was bored; it was not enough for him to take in hand the farms at Windsor and make a success of them. He was serious-minded, with intellectual interests and an accomplished musician – not at all the English aristocracy's kind of man, a hard-drinking, hard rider to hounds, etc. He took up public issues and quietly inserted himself into politics *pour faute de mieux* – always under the guise of advising his self-willed consort, who came to depend on him and found she could dispense with dear Lord Melbourne. The latter one day let out that 'the Prince is bored with the sameness of his chess every evening. He would like to bring literary and scientific people about the Court, vary the society and infuse a more useful tendency into it. The Queen, however, has no fancy to encourage such people. This arises from a feeling on her part that her education has not fitted her to take part in such conversation; she would not like conversation to be going on in which she could not take her fair share.'

In short, tiny as she was, she meant to dominate the whole show, and succeeded in doing so, to an extraordinary degree, to the very end of her long life. 'The Queen is very proud of the Prince's utter indifference to the attractions of all ladies.' It may be said that there were some sides of life which were to her a closed book. 'I think she is a little jealous of his talking much even to men.' It must have been suffocating: no wonder he displayed not much will to live and just gave up – a great loss to the country – at forty-two.

However, he did his duty and gave her a large family, much as the Queen objected to child-bearing – she seems to have thought it the fault of the men-folk – and didn't like children. In default of intellectual interests there was the growing family. In December 1841, she is writing, 'we arrived here *sains et saufs* with our awfully large Nursery Establishment. We walked out early and felt like prisoners freed from some dungeon.' This was a month after the birth of Albert Edward, the future Edward VII. The eldest children experienced the severe side of the Queen's nature. In 1858 Baron Stockmar went down to Windsor to discuss their treatment with Prince Albert, whom Stockmar described as 'completely cowed' and in terror 'lest the Queen's mind should be excited by any opposition to her will. The Prince of Wales resented very much the severity which he had experienced.' So also Vicky, the Princess Royal: she and her father took refuge in each other. It must be admitted that, after his death, her attitude to the children, even towards the disapproved-of, naughty Bertie, underwent a change. Even Queen Victoria developed with the years.

Then there were the visiting royalties, and the innumerable European ramifications of the family – it became practically a full time job in itself and involved her in an enormous correspondence. In 1842 came over the King of Prussia, a common-looking corpulent fellow and a great glutton, for the christening of Albert Edward. He stayed at Windsor, but went up to town every day for public functions. He was much struck with 'the grandeur and magnificence both at Court and elsewhere' – one is reminded of Marshal Blücher's

Overleaf: The christening of Prince Edward (later Edward VII) in St George's Chapel 1841.

first impression of the City, '*Was für Plunder!*' Greville notes that Melbourne was hardly ever at the Castle now – Victoria had her man; with his insight into her character, Melbourne was sure that Albert would gain an intellectual ascendancy over her. By 1842 the Council went regularly down by special train – Greville found the 'velocity delightful'. On one occasion the Tory Lord Chancellor Lyndhurst 'began a sort of dancing movement in the drawing-room ... seventy years of age, ten years of idleness, and a young wife will not do for the labour of the Great Seal'. Greville thought the Lord Chancellor not long for this world – actually he lasted a further twenty years.

In 1844 there was an unexpected descent of the Czar Nicholas. The Queen writes that she gave 'every evening a large dinner in the Waterloo Room, the last two evenings in uniforms, as the Emperor disliked so being *en frac* and was quite embarrassed in it'. He too, like most of these Royals, was a German after all. He had so friendly a reception in England that he seems to have thought he could get away with dividing up the Turkish Empire, with Britain's connivance – which led to the Crimean War. It was memories of the common struggle against Napoleon that gave the Czar his popularity. Wellington attired himself as a Russian Field-Marshal to receive him, and there was a Review at Windsor: 'the sight was pretty, glorious weather, 4,000 Guards, Horse, Foot and Artillery in the Park, the Queen *en calèche* with a brilliant suite'. The old Duke put himself at the head of his regiment once more, to march past Queen and Emperor, who then rode up to shake his hand.

With French royalties Waterloo had to be kept in the background: no parties in the Chamber for Louis Philippe, but he was invested with the Garter, for which occasion the full ceremonial was revived after the lapse of years. He was highly pleased – the contrast with his years of penury in England during the Revolution must have struck him – and was enchanted with the Castle.

For Napoleon III's visit in 1855 the Waterloo Chamber was renamed the Picture Gallery; this was during the Crimean War, in which the English and French were now allies against an overbearing Russia. Everybody was nervous at this Napoleonic invasion of Windsor, none more so than the Emperor himself, while the Empress Eugénie, 'fearful of the Queen not liking her', stood up in the carriage at the sight of Victoria greeting her at the door. We have a description of it all from the celebrated Bishop Wilberforce, Soapy Sam. 'The Emperor rather mean-looking, small, and a tendency to *embonpoint*; a remarkable way of swimming up a room with an uncertain gait; a small grey eye, looking cunning, but with an aspect of softness about it too.' (It is highly doubtful whether he had any Bonaparte blood at all, his mother Hortense, Queen of Holland, having been no better than she should be.) As Prelate of the Order Wilberforce took part in a very full Chapter, at which the Emperor was

Bishop
Wilberforce –
'Soapy Sam'.

installed and said to him, 'This is a remarkable event in my life.' It was hardly less remarkable for the Duke of Buckingham, who came unsummoned and was not asked to remain to dinner – the expense of Stowe had bankrupted him.

The Prince of Wales's confirmation is described by the Queen to her daughter, then Crown Princess of Prussia. 'I wore a blue *moire antique* made thus [quite good at sketching, she drew the design], the body trimmed with blue ribbon, white silk with *guipure* lace over it. The lace is off the Empress's dressing-gown [which Eugénie, Queen of fashion and all the resources of Worth's at command, must have given her]. Bertie wore his Windsor uniform, Alice in blue silk, light and dark stripes, Lenchen [the family name for Helena] and Louise in blue silk small stripes, trimmed with black velvet. Alfred and Arthur in Highland dress. I wore the brooch of you as a little angel.' We are grateful for this glimpse of the feminine side of the Queen's mind. Then came the serious part of the affair: 'the Archbishop made a very good and impressive charge, pointing out the duties of a Christian'. Unfortunately, from this time Bertie's naughtinesses began, culminating with his entanglement with a girl at Cambridge, where the Prince Consort caught his fatal cold. Though the drains at Windsor may have been as much to blame, the Queen held Bertie in disfavour for some years. This was at any rate in the Hanoverian family tradition, and was to recur with George v and his heir, the later Duke of Windsor.

Christmas 1860 was the Prince Consort's last, and the last gay Christmas at Windsor for the rest of the century. It was very cold and frosty but sunny, with the younger members of the family playing ice-hockey. Among the guests the aged Palmerston represented the past, Mr Disraeli the future. Princess Alice was to be married; the latter readily agreed that the state should provide a dowry of £30,000 with an annuity of £3,000. But that year Albert was not well, and had a presentiment that he would die. He was desperately ill when the serious crisis over the *Trent* blew up with the United States, now in the grip of the Civil War. Palmerston had drafted an aggressive dispatch, which might have involved this country in war; the Prince Consort spent his last strength in redrafting the Note, toning it down and making accommodation possible. It was his last service to the state. In December he was moved into the room in which William iv had last seen the sun of Waterloo day set, and there 14 December 1861 Albert died. 'Will they do him justice now?' Victoria said, looking for the last time on his face. The rest of her life she dedicated to his memory – and to carrying out her duty as she conceived he would have wished her.

Four days after his death she went to Frogmore to choose a spot for a mausoleum where she and Albert and other members of the family would be together. Meanwhile his body lay in George iii's vault. A year later he was re-interred,

Left: Christmas at Windsor – Victoria and Albert with their family.

after a service in the room where he died, his bust on the bed and flowers all round it. The inevitable Bishop Wilberforce performed the ceremony: 'I am just home from the consecration of the mausoleum', he wrote from the Castle: 'one of the most touching scenes I ever saw, to see our Queen and the fatherless children walk in and kneel down in those solemn prayers. I had a half-hour's talk with her yesterday and nothing could be more delightful, so gentle, so affectionate, so true, so real – no touch of morbidness – quite cheerful and so kind.' One sees how the good Bishop came by his *soubriquet*.

Victoria had been optimistic to the end in her reports on Albert's illness to Uncle Leopold: 'I *had* hoped with such instinctive certainty that God never *would* part us.' Albert had no such certainty or indeed any will to live; hers was merely a reflection of her own exceptional vitality – hence too the egoism which kept her going. We draw a veil over her unceasing lamentations about her fate, the voluminous and variegated expressions of her grief – as if no-one else had ever lost a husband. It is true enough, as the editor of her Letters points out, that there was a regular Victorian cult of death, of which the Queen was the most conspicuous exponent. But, with her extravagance of temperament, she overdid it: there was, as Coleridge said of the Germans, 'a nimiety, a too-muchness' about her.

Enough on that subject. It is relevant here to point out, however, that from that time her attitude towards Windsor underwent a change. We hear no more about its being prison-like and gloomy: it had become a shrine, and with that the real centre of the family life and cult.

We may pause at this dividing point in the long reign, to note the appearance in its early years of the most popular contribution to the prose-literature of Windsor. People had tired of the inanities of the 'fashionable novel', and Harrison Ainsworth had found with his *Tower of London* a formula combining chronicle-history with romance, which greatly appealed to the Victorian public. In 1843 he published his *Windsor Castle*; though without the sombre drama of his book about the Tower, it had similar qualities to recommend it, vividness and freshness of descriptive power, a good grasp of history, with an admixture of sentiment.

In the middle of the book there was a useful summary of the Castle's history for Victorian readers, and for us revealing of the inflexion and sympathies of the age. None of the Georgian enthusiasm for Benjamin West's work in St George's Chapel. Ainsworth chimed with Victorian taste in urging its removal and the replacement of the tracery. This was ultimately done, with a dull Clayton and Bell window in memory of the Prince Consort. We learn that the great west window nearly shared the fate of the east: this would have

Right: The east window reconstructed in memory of Prince Albert.

been a terrible loss, for the glass is mainly of the sixteenth century; Blore was content to restore the tracery. Ainsworth questioned Wyatville's destruction of Hugh May's chapel and rightly thought the enlarged St George's Hall too big. He argued for the removal of the interesting old houses around the Chapel and the clutter against the Castle walls. In all this Ainsworth was a precursor of Victorian taste and what he advocated came about, as with his suggestions for improvements at the Tower.

A whole chapter is given to 'The Legend of Herne the Hunter', an elaboration of the folklore Shakespeare made use of in *The Merry Wives of Windsor*, and making use of the old proverb, 'A hurt from hart's horn bringeth to the bier.' This again supplied material for a Windsor contribution to another art, Vaughan Williams' opera, *Sir John in Love*.

John Brown – the Scottish Highlander who served Queen Victoria.
Drawing by K. MacLear, 1866.

Until the fatal year 1861 there had usually been plays at Windsor for Christmas – we hear of Charles Kean producing *The Merchant of Venice* in the Rubens Room in 1848. After 1861 Victoria gives herself more sedately to reading. She did not much care for reading novels, but those of Mrs Oliphant or Mrs Craik were read aloud to her with approbation. For herself she much preferred poetry: 'poems I am fond of in all shapes'. She had been consoled by Tennyson's dedicating the second edition of *Idylls of the King* to the memory of her own beloved:

> We know him now: all narrow jealousies
> Are silent; and we see him as he moved,
> How modest, kindly, all-accomplished, wise,
> With what sublime repression of himself . . .

We find her struggling with his more 'difficult' poems, but what she really liked was luxuriating in grief, like Elizabeth Barrett Browning:

> As one alone, once not alone,
> I sit and knock at Nature's door,
> Heart-bare, heart-hungry, very poor,
> Whose desolated days go on.

Albert, however, was at rest from his labours. When Sir Edwin Landseer came to see her for the first time since the Prince's death, 'he cried dreadfully'. It is the world of Edward Lear or of 'The Walrus and the Carpenter'. Now the Queen is reading the controversial Kinglake, with his strictures on the conduct of the Crimean War: 'it is very scurrilous. I go daily to the beloved Mausoleum, and long to be there!' Charles Kingsley comes to preach and much appeals to the Queen's Scottish *schwärmerei* by saying that the 'English peasantry had not a grain of poetry in their nature whereas the Scotch are full of it!' Mrs Kingsley, a quintessential Victorian, comments on his reception at Windsor, 'from that hour to his dying day he received marks of Royal kindness and condescension, the memory of which will be an heirloom to his children'. What was of more practical importance was that, from this time, the attacks on Parson Lot's earlier Radicalism piped down.

Shortly Queen Victoria's Scotch sympathies received a notable accession of strength by recruiting Highland John Brown to her service. When he first attended the anniversary service at 'the dear Mausoleum' and 'came to my room later, he was so much affected. He said in his simple, expressive way, with such a tender look of pity while the tears rolled down his cheeks, "I didn't like to see ye at Frogmore this morning. I felt for ye, to see ye coming there with your daughters and your husband lying there – marriage on one side and death on the other. I felt sorry for ye. I feel for ye, but what can I do for ye? I could die for ye."' It is hardly surprising that the Queen decided to make him her personal out-of-doors attendant – 'he is so devoted and attached, and clever and so wonderfully able to interpret one's wishes . . . whose only object and interest is my service, and God knows how I want so much to be taken care of.'

Duty called, and in 1863 there was the wedding of the Prince of Wales to the lovely Alexandra from Denmark: this was a love-match and 'dear Alix' always a favourite with her redoubtable mother-in-law. Vicky was to have rooms in the Devil's Tower, and 'dear William' – who, as the Kaiser, was to give her so much concern and the world so much trouble – 'will be in the dear old nursery where he will have every possible comfort and watching'. We have a glimpse of that March day from the unaccustomed eyes of an Eton boy who was to become the father of Sir Winston Churchill, Lord Randolph. 'We all mustered in the school-yard and then marched up Windsor into the Castle by Henry VIII's gate.' The first procession was that of the King of Denmark, then came the Princess Royal (Vicky). 'She bowed away as hard as she could go – I think her neck must have been stiff. And then came the Prince.' At the drive to the station the boy got right up to the carriage-door, shouting 'Hurrah!', while the Prince bowed back. It was an ironical fore-shadowing of the controversial relations that these two were subsequently to enjoy.*

The Marlboroughs were much put out that they were not asked to St George's Chapel, while the Disraelis were. But there was a more serious awkwardness than this; for meanwhile the Schleswig-Holstein crisis had blown up, and all the Danish royal family were on one side, while the Prussian were on the other. Though Vicky was regarded in Germany, with characteristic spite, as *die Engländerin*, she stood loyally with the Hohenzollerns she had married into. The tragedy of her life was that she and her husband the Crown Prince Frederick knew that Germany was set on an ultimately disastrous course by Bismarck, and they could do nothing about it. She wrote, 'my daily prayer and the labour of my life is that Fritz [her husband] should make those principles his own [responsible, constitutional government], which are the only ones which can alone be the saving – not only of Prussia's position in Europe and in Germany – but of the Prussian monarchy'.

Thus Queen Victoria's intelligent daughter: how precisely right she was should have been brought home to her son in 1918. The lesson was lost on the Germans, so that a still more calamitous lesson was needed in our time.

The civilised alternative to Bismarck was Mr Gladstone: to the 'blood and

---

* cf. my *The Later Churchills*, c. IX.

Vicky and Fritz – Victoria's daughter and her husband, Crown
Prince Frederick of Prussia on their honeymoon, 1858.

iron', the brute force and blackmail of the one was opposed the liberal ideal of self-government of the other. The contrast was well appreciated at the time, and neither Bismarck nor Gladstone could bear the other. Nor could Queen Victoria, her daughter, or her intelligent mother-in-law, the old Empress Augusta, stand Bismarck: the instinct of these women was right: they recognised a brute of genius.

We find Mr Gladstone entertained at the Castle, still more at the Deanery, for he was very churchy. The disestablishment of the Irish Church was the beginning of the Queen's increasing disaccord with Gladstone. Bishop Wilberforce records dining at Windsor in 1869, 'the Queen very affable. "So sorry Mr Gladstone started this about the Irish Church, and he is a great friend of yours", etc.' This was a dig at their both being High Church, for the Queen was quite as aggressively Protestant as any of her Hanoverian forbears.

In Dean Wellesley, Wellington's nephew, the Queen had a leading ecclesiastical adviser, 'our best friend', for close on thirty years. He was excessively Low Church – preaching in the royal chapels was in a black gown; a surplice was thought High Church, so was *Hymns Ancient and Modern*. Dean Randall Davidson succeeded to this confidential position – what, in a Catholic monarch, would have been that of a confessor. 'The appointment of Dean of Windsor would go through the Prime Minister, but it is *understood* I should select him.' His wife would be a great asset, having been born in the purple, daughter of Archbishop Tait: especially at Windsor, 'which is a place of rather a gossiping nature, requiring tact and Judgment'. The only objection was on the ground of the new Dean's youth: he would have to preside over a Chapter of old fossils. Mr Gladstone put it with his unfailing courtesy: 'you will preside in a Chapter over most of whose members you have so much the advantage in point of age, with a courtesy and consideration which will show the circle of your gifts is complete'. It was – and he ended up as Archbishop of Canterbury.

Almost at once his 'tact and Judgment' were tried by a collision with the Queen over her intention to publish yet *More Leaves from the Journal of a Life in the Highlands*. She had done it twice before, and was rather innocently proud of her success as a best-seller. She had not noticed the silence of her family, and she was not in a position to know the mirth her self-exposure had given rise to among the sophisticated and unkind. Now there was the threat of a third, with who knows what sentimentalities about John Brown? The Dean thought it his duty to warn her that 'there are, especially among the humbler classes, some, (perhaps it would be true to say *many*) whose spirit, judging by their published periodicals, is one of such unappreciative criticism as I should not desire your Majesty to see'.

The Queen was thunderstruck at such sentiments, very surprised at her Dean,

Right: Albert's mausoleum at Frogmore.
Overleaf: The throne room: Queen Victoria with her Knights of the Garter.

and let it be known that of course she would publish the book. Now Davidson showed what a brave man he was: there was no-one else who would tell her and he was determined to save her from ridicule. He wrote a second letter, putting the point more strongly and said he would continue to ask her to desist. She was furious, and asked him to withdraw or at least apologise. Instead, he wrote a third letter adhering to what he knew was right, and offered his resignation. There was a fortnight's complete silence – she could not bear discussion, let alone contradiction. When she saw him again she was friendlier than ever and reposed complete confidence in him from that time forth. No more was heard of the book.

The episode does credit to them both, though most of all, one must own without gallantry, to the man. On her side she recognised a man of courage and a good man when she saw one: the future Archbishop was both.

When young Davidson came to reside at Windsor the Queen was sixty-four; with his exceptional perception his penetration into her personality is at once most acute and just. She had a powerful combination of strong 'common sense, persistent industry, genuine and whole-hearted devotion to duty, and affectionate sympathy with people who were in trouble'. He could not define the 'irresistible charm' there was for those who knew her best – rather lacking in the public image; but it clearly came from her openness of nature, her transparent sincerity and honesty of heart and mind. We can all appreciate that better now that her private letters to her daughter Vicky have been laid open to view. There was, however, one great difficulty for one in her position: she disliked any direct confrontation – she 'disliked contradicting as much as being contradicted'.

Here was, perhaps, a defect that attaches to very high breeding in a Court – though it never reached the Chinese obliqueness of Louis xv's Versailles, where hardly anything unpleasant could be directly referred to. When Madame de Pompadour's body was being taken away to be buried on a night of bad weather, the only comment the King could permit himself, watching from a window, was – 'Madame will have an ill journey tonight.'

When something came up that was unpleasant Queen Victoria would not go into it, but end the conversation and then write a note about it or make someone else reprove the fault she had observed. When a young lady-in-waiting appeared rather heavily made up, the Queen said, 'Dear General Grey will tell her.' When the message came to him, he was heard to murmur, 'Dear General Grey will do nothing of the kind.' It is a tribute to the toughness of her common sense that it came through in such circumstances, the integrity of her judgment intact. Her Private Secretary, Sir Henry Ponsonby, was in fact a Liberal, a good friend to Mr Gladstone. Fortunately for him in his situation he had a

Above left: The approach to the castle from the Great Park.
Below left: The great west window of St George's Chapel.

sense of humour; but Davidson thought that his one defect was a want of courage. Like the Prince Consort, he would never stand up to the Queen when he thought she was wrong. Ponsonby found the youthful Dean a pillar of support in awkwardnesses that arose, not only Church questions, though here is one: 'Do we officially believe in Purgatory? Canon Lucock of Ely wrote a book about the future state. He apparently knows all about it. He states that the Queen has expressed herself warmly in favour of his book (??). And so wants to send another.' We get a glimpse of the nonsense public persons have to put up with from silly people.

Our best close-up of the way of life at Windsor comes from Ponsonby's letters. He was the son of a Waterloo veteran who had led an heroic charge, been left for dead on the battlefield, but recovered. His son, the Secretary, was punctilious in normally dating his letters, but, when he came to 18 June, it was always with him 'Waterloo Day' – we see something of the cult it was in that century. The Ponsonbys inhabited the Norman Tower and made an interesting hospitable dwelling of it, with log-fires to keep out the cold. (The Queen hated fires and thought them unhealthy; at Balmoral everybody shivered.) Lord Ronald Gower, with his antiquarian tastes – he wrote a book on the Tower of London – approved of what Lady Ponsonby had done with the Norman Tower, turning the dungeon room into her study: 'the old walls with the inscriptions by prisoners confined here in Cromwell's time had been hidden by lath and plaster and wall papers'.

The Ponsonby children found the Moat a fine place to play in and thought the place belonged to them. They had friends among the canons and their children at St George's, where the music was notably good under Sir Walter Parratt and maintained a cathedral standard. (Poor Archbishop Laud had won by his martyrdom at the hand of the horrid Puritans.) Sometimes the children were taken to the private chapel, where Queen Victoria was stationed up in the gallery: they were forbidden to look up, but invariably did. The preacher up in the pulpit found himself on a level with the Queen, 'whose unflagging attention was more often accompanied by a look of disapproval than of appreciation'. However, she did not interrupt, as Elizabeth I did: 'To your text, Master Preacher, to your text.' (But he had been commenting infelicitously on her advancing years.) Victoria did not cherish the memory of her great prede-cessor – 'So unkind to my ancestress, the Queen of Scots.' With her Stuart sentiment Victoria collected a whole cabinet of relics at Windsor, including the gold travelling dinner-service of the Cardinal of York, the last Stuart Pretender.

One of the Chapter was the loud-voiced Canon Dalton, who had been tutor to Edward VII's sons and served again to instruct the Duke of Windsor in the mysteries of the Faith, of which he notes that he was to become 'Defender' –

though only for a short period. The Duke describes him as being as craggy as the Castle itself. Ponsonby was given the task of handing him one of her Majesty's messages: 'As Tutor Mr Dalton never said Grace, but as Canon he does and she hears has done so in Latin. Pray tell him it must be in English and only *one*.' His son grew up to be a leading Socialist politician, with an unpopular personality. In his own Autobiography he had to correct the popular legend that he had said as a child, 'Go away, Queen, I'm eating cake', and that she had commented, 'What a horrid little boy!' He probably was, but all she had said was, 'What a loud voice that child has, just like his father!' This, as the House of Commons well knew, was no more than the truth: he bellowed. At Windsor, in the Queen's presence, everybody was supposed to whisper.

There was the constant coming and going of leading political figures, for Windsor was the seat of authority, an indispensable wheel in the machine of government and this was the closest the Queen would come to it. There was a certain republicanism expressed as the result of her refusal to live in London. This made her indignant: 'excepting Balls and parties and going to Theatres and living in town the Queen *neglected nothing* . . . when morally and physically she is doing much more than she can bear with her overwhelming work. She never went out into general Society before '61 and never would have done it.' In fact she disapproved of smart light-hearted society – she knew how heartless it was and thought that it set no good example. Her own tastes were simple and dignified, and not in the least vulgar. She hated ostentation and display: 'crowns and pageantry may have been necessary for other monarchs'; for her they were not. 'In this her point of view was quite original. So the bonnet triumphed: she wore it at both her jubilees.' The utmost she would go was to wear, at indoor functions, a little diamond crown and the Garter ribbon. In the long run her instinct was right: her homeliness endeared her to her peoples and the modest, if jewelled, mourning made a far more appealing symbol across her far-flung Empire.

Her relations with Mr Gladstone were good up to his disestablishment of the Irish Church; but as he waded further into the deeps of Home Rule and overflowed the country with demagogic oratory her mistrust grew to detestation. She was convinced that Mr G. was the victim of his own delusions: 'he can convince himself black is white and wrong is right – which makes him so dangerous'. With that prince of casuists, trained in the Oxford Greats School, she certainly had a point; and her retentive memory recalled what Palmerston had said to her, ' "he is a very dangerous man." No one can be sure for a moment what he may *persuade himself* to think right, and hence the impossibility to place confidence in him.'

Now Mr Disraeli was far more deft in handling her, and Ponsonby saw perfectly how it was done. 'He communicates nothing except boundless professions of love and loyalty, and if called on to write more says he is ill.' Here was an example: there had been a bomb-attempt upon the Czar in 1879; at once Disraeli, 'this Russian catastrophe makes me nervous . . . I hope, there-fore, indeed I feel sure, that you are taking all due precautions about the move-ments of our Sovereign Lady, whether in walks or rides, and that you have adequate experts hovering over the towers and terraces of Windsor.' Ponsonby: 'he has got the length of her foot exactly and knows how to be sympathetic. You and I know that his sympathy is expressed with his tongue in his cheek. But are not her woes told in the same manner?'

Windsor, 1894 – the Queen, Princess Louis of Battenberg and Princess Henry of Prussia. John Brown is on the right, the Munshi on the left.

Ponsonby considered Disraeli a cleverer man than Gladstone with 'his terrible earnestness' – and utter humourlessness, he might have added. Among the lesser fry of politicians there was a Henry Fowler, later Lord Wolverhampton (fancy choosing such a title!). He was the first Wesleyan to become a Cabinet minister, and was very touchy at not receiving the accolade of an invitation 'to dine and sleep'. He fancied a slight, and would refer to it as 'the Windsor boycott'. He got no sympathy from the aristocratic soul of his chief, Lord Salisbury, who set no store by such things (he didn't need to). Nor was the heir to all the Cavendishes intimidated by the ritual of Windsor. The Queen ate little and fast, and the custom was to remove the plates when she had finished. The Duke of Devonshire was a slow eater, and when he noticed his unfinished dinner being whisked away by a flunkey, he called out sharply, 'Here! bring that back.'

Among the younger generation the Curzons may be said to have won the label, 'Approved, V. R. I.'. (Dizzy had made her Empress of India. Henceforth there were always Indian servants in attendance. The impassive Munshi, always there, came to take the place of John Brown – the entourage thought his mysterious, impenetrable figure, silent and statuesque, a spy.) The Sovereign Lady found young Mr Curzon 'clever and agreeable', his rich American bride, 'an American from Washington, very handsome and ladylike'. Lord Randolph Churchill was not approved, and no wonder: he chose to resign from Lord Salisbury's government while a guest at Windsor, without a hint of it to the Queen in the course of a long conversation, sending in his resignation on her writing paper. To his surprise it was accepted – it was the end of his meteoric career.

Gradually the gloom that had descended with the Prince Consort's death was alleviated: since the Queen would not go to entertainments in London, actors and singers were summoned to Windsor, where a stage could be put up in the Waterloo Gallery. In the course of years entertainments became a regular feature of Court life. Shakespeare returned to Windsor once more, though not *The Merry Wives*. Tennyson's *Becket*, to be performed by Sir Henry Irving, offered rather a problem, as the Prince of Wales and Prince George (of all people!) found some very strong language in it, 'disagreeable and coarse' rather; and Princess Louise found one scene very 'awkward'. 'The Queen hates anything of that sort.' There followed some rather comic correspondence: Ponsonby could not see anything very objectionable in it, 'though the language is sometimes strong – as is natural. He has written to Lord Tennyson as desired by Your Majesty.'

Sublimely unaware, permission was given to Mr Oscar Wilde to report the memorial service for the Emperor William I in 1888, for the *Daily Telegraph*. Mr Wilde was allowed into St George's Chapel, where he found himself 'most affected'. Next year the young Kaiser was anxious to come and be received by his grandmother at Windsor. But he had behaved like the bounder – to use a Victorian word – he was. Much worse, in fact, to his mother, whose husband had succeeded as Emperor Frederick, twenty years too late, when dying of cancer. Young William allied himself with the reactionary tribe in Germany who hated Frederick and his wife for their Liberal and constitutional sympathies. On his death the palace was surrounded by troops to prevent his widow getting her papers out of the country. Three boxes of them had already been safely deposited at Windsor. Her son's behaviour to his mother and his father's memory, inspired by the Bismarcks, had nothing of Coburg about it: it was of a Prussian brutality. The appropriate comment was that of honest John Brown, who had known the bumptious Kaiser since he was a child: he said he wanted a 'good skelping'.

William sent over to Windsor a Prussian general who made no secret of his satisfaction at the Emperor Frederick's death. Queen Victoria well knew how to deal with that sort of impertinence – her granddaughter, Princess Marie Louise, once told me of the ice-cold stare of those china-blue eyes that could quell anybody. Of course the new Emperor complained of his emissary's reception. The missive was minuted by her: 'The Queen intended it should be cold. She last saw him as her son-in-law's A D C. He never uttered one word of sorrow for his death, and rejoiced in the accession of his new master.' The new master was anxious to come over and show himself off as Emperor, but grandmama did not wish to see him at Windsor. The sensible old lady wrote, 'we have always been very intimate with our grandson, and to pretend that he is to be treated *in private* as in public as "His Imperial Majesty" is *perfect madness*!' In addition the young man was opposing a Battenberg love-match for Princess Beatrice as a *mésalliance* – at which the Queen was rightly indignant: she was totally above and beyond being a snob.

The Kaiser insisted on coming, and was received at Osborne, where he was soothed by being made an Admiral of the Fleet. 'Fancy wearing the same uniform as St Vincent and Nelson! It is enough to make me quite giddy!' That is the word for it – just what he was. His ambivalent feelings about England, the love-hate complex, the sense of inferiority compensating itself by boasting and threats, the inflamed jealousy with the impossible longing to be appreciated – all that chimed with the dominant mood of the parvenu German Empire: that was what made it so dangerous. In the grandiose Schloss in Berlin I have seen in the Kaiser's study his desk made from the timbers of Nelson's *Victory*, the whole place now levelled with the ground.

On this visit his grandmother tried to persuade him to treat his mother better, without much success; and, still giddy, he made a speech in Germany saying he would have all the Social Democrats shot down. However, ten years later, in the crisis of the Boer War, the Kaiser behaved noticeably better and was rewarded with a state-visit to Windsor. Everything was laid on for him – at the banquet in St George's Hall 'the entire service of the table was gold, all the candelabra and decorations of gold, and three huge screens of velvet were covered with platters and every imaginable piece in gold – in fact, all that the Queen possesses'. This country was then not only the first country in the world, but the richest.

The long reign was coming to an end. The usual unvarying ritual was kept up to the last. Bishop Creighton describes the Queen at a family birthday party for the Prince of Wales: 'She is a little old woman, very much crippled in the legs with rheumatism, walking with a stick and leaning on her Indian attendant, who was clad in a turban and a magnificent Oriental dress.' Creighton noticed particularly her beautiful voice, which everyone paid tribute to – it was deep and resonant, like Mary Tudor, quite unlike Elizabeth I. Lord Ronald Gower was at Windsor again in March 1898, within three years of the end: 'The Queen much bent, her Majesty held out her hand to me; I passed round the Duchess of Roxburghe's chair, knelt and kissed her hand, which was rather a difficult feat to perform.' Seated in the corridor the old lady was 'as animated as ever', glittering with jewels and fingers covered with rings – but her hand shook. How long ago since those first days when the young Queen would ride out in her flowing habit into the Great Park, Lord Melbourne beside her, the splendid retinue following behind!

Next day Lord Ronald found 'brilliantly sunny and Windsor looking its best, which is saying much'. After prayers in the private chapel read by the Dean, 'I was struck when alone in the Armoury by the glamour of that hall. Nelson's bust by Chantrey, placed on the fragment of the mast of the *Victory*; the busts of Wellington and Marlborough, and before one the great round Keep of the Castle, the Royal Standard fluttering proudly over it, a glorious blue sky over all.' The year before had been the Diamond Jubilee; Albert's *Te Deum* had been sung once again at St George's, then the Queen and the Empress Frederick had slipped away to their devotions at the Mausoleum.

The Boer War gnawed away at the old woman's strength, though her courage and devotion to duty were as great as ever. The succession of disasters with which the war began gave her the deepest anxiety; one day Lord Esher saw her turn pale when a telegram was handed to her during dinner – she said it made her ill. But her spirit rose to meet the crisis; she redoubled her efforts to encourage everybody, especially her soldiers. Kipling, the laureate of the war, responded on behalf of the soldiery with 'The Widow of Windsor'. She was indefatigable in inspecting troops; messages of encouragement went out

all over the Empire, of condolence to the bereaved. At Christmas 1899 she gave up her Osborne holiday to entertain wives and children of non-commissioned officers at Windsor. When the tide of disaster in South Africa turned she led the national feeling of relief, came to London and for two days drove through miles of streets, returning thanks.

Most of April 1900 she spent in Dublin, her first visit for forty years – really an acknowledgment of the splendid service of her Irish troops in the war. Now eighty she returned to a very busy year, military inspections and reviews, visits to hospitals, state-visits of the King of Sweden and the Khedive of Egypt, the usual Court-entertainments at Windsor; she even held a Drawing-Room at Buckingham Palace. There were the increasingly numerous family gatherings, christenings and bereavements. By the end of the year she was worn out. Taken ill at Windsor, she indomitably held a Council and inspected wounded Colonial troops indoors in St George's Hall. In December she moved to Osborne where she died next month, 22 January 1901. The new King and the Kaiser lifted the child's-body, through whom they had come into the world, into her coffin. On its way uphill on the journey home to Windsor, a horse snapped the traces of the gun-carriage; a contingent of her sailors dragged the carriage with the tiny coffin into the Castle.

So long a reign, the continuity broken at last, gave a great shock – few people could remember when she had not been there. Indeed, it is extraordinary to think that there lived and reigned into this century a sovereign who was only a granddaughter of George III – and her grandfather had reigned over the American Colonies before ever the United States came into existence.

Left: Queen Victoria's funeral procession makes its way to the mausoleum at Frogmore.

8
Edwardian and Georgian Epilogue

IT is said that, when Queen Alexandra knelt to kiss the new King's hand, Edward said, in his guttural German: '*Es ist zu spät.*' But it was not too late for him to set a completely new style in his brief reign. Lord Esher, who had been a favourite with the old Queen and was to remain so with Edward VII, depicts in his Diaries the immediate change of atmosphere at Windsor. No longer the hush of the Queen's dinners, when everybody spoke in a whisper; no longer the Indian servants, silent, immobile, statuesque – they wandered round the Castle like lost spirits. The mysterious Munshi disappeared. Esher noted that, with the all too human Edward, the *mystique* had gone: 'the sanctity of the throne has disappeared'.

Esher observed the new monarch, hat jauntily on his head, cigar in mouth, dogs at his heels, charging through the rooms of the Castle, turning out cupboards, disturbing old accumulations, emptying drawers, distributing photographs, re-arranging things for comfort and convenience. Queen Alexandra wanted to live in the State Apartments; Edward would have none of that, he insisted on his parents' old rooms – but they acquired a very different atmosphere. Interested always in appearances and dress, he appointed a 'nice' new uniform for Esher – blue and scarlet with a sash – who was made Deputy Governor of the Castle with the 'right of pit and gallows'. Esher himself was a man of taste, and spent mornings in the Royal Library studying the wonderful collection of miniatures – there was Monmouth, 'who was a real beauty'. Esher was well capable of appreciating that, less engaged by Nell Gwyn 'practically naked'. Every man to his taste. The King's was for women: there was a grand ball at which the beautiful Mrs Keppel wore a train so excessively long that it tripped up Prince Adolphus and Princess Victoria.

Where the old Queen had been the dynastic pivot of Northern Europe, Edward was the unchallenged social centre. In June 1903 he gave a ball to which a thousand guests were invited, and this was not a state occasion but a private party – there had been no such thing at Windsor for sixty years. Next month

The royal gathering at Windsor, November 17, 1907. *Left to right:* Queen of Norway, King of Spain, German Emperor, German Empress, Queen Alexandra, Queen of Portugal, King Edward and Queen of Spain.

there was a ball for the President of the French Republic, with a hundred French senators; in the autumn galas for the King of Italy. When the next French President came, a more demotic type, 'he took more interest in the fat cattle and the gardens than in the Castle itself'. John Morley, who – though a Radical, was a historian and a cultivated man – was enchanted: 'at last, at Windsor, I feel myself in a palace'. Even under Edward VII there were intellectual entertainments of a sort. Barrie's *Quality Street* was beautifully acted: the King thought it pretty but lacking in strength (he had a point there). Then Barrie came to read two new one-act plays in the Green Library – they were acclaimed 'wonderfully good'. And there was Elgar as Master of the King's Musick: that was something.

There was always the problem posed by King Edward's nephew, the Kaiser. Determined on a state-visit, he wanted to give it political overtones by bringing his Chancellor, the false and disingenuous Bülow. This would have created an unfavourable impression in France, now an ally – which was of course the intention. In the event he brought Eulenburg, who was a good friend to peace; for this his career was ruined and himself framed, in familiar German manner, on charges of homosexuality.

Everything was laid on to sweeten William. There was a great banquet, a finer spectacle than had ever been seen in St George's Hall, with the juxtaposition of the Middle Ages and the twentieth century: all the gold out, and lines of beefeaters in their gorgeous dress specially brought from the Tower. It made the Kaiser only the more envious and, nervous, he created a bad impression by a vehement anti-Jewish outburst. (His uncle was pro-Jewish and had close friends like Sir Ernest Cassel and the Rothschilds.) The Kaiser said, 'there are far too many of them in my country. They want stamping out.' He did not improve matters by insisting on talking politics – in resentment against the Anglo-French Entente, which Germany herself had done most to bring about. Lord Lansdowne, the *grand seigneur* who had effected the alliance, described the Kaiser's criticisms of Lord Salisbury and Joseph Chamberlain (who had been ignorantly anxious for a German alliance) as 'gross incivility'. His uncle's Foreign Secretary, Sir Edward Grey, the Kaiser condescendingly described as 'a capable sort of country gentleman'. Esher comments, 'the effrontery of the man!' However, Grey saw the Kaiser out.

Edward had gathered twenty-four royalties, with the Kings and Queens of Spain and Norway, at the farewell lunch for his nephew, to do him honour (and perhaps to put him in his place). There was no doubt *who* was the social centre of Europe; Esher tells us how glad Uncle Bertie was to see his nephew off.

A connoisseur and something of a scholar, Esher was fascinated by the royal family as an historian, noticing family affinities and hereditary traits. He was given the job of going through Queen Victoria's private journals – fancy her finding time to keep them, on top of everything else! – it shows what a worker she was. Their decreed destruction constituted a sad loss to the historian. In her day members of the royal family were not allowed to roam about the Castle, with the result that many of them did not know their way about in it. Edward VII made precipitate, and rather Philistine changes, which Queen Mary subsequently disapproved, having more taste. But when her husband, who became George V, went down to Windsor in his father's régime, he found that it was much more comfortable and there was altogether more *room*.

One day Esher was left in charge of George's children, the future Edward VIII and George VI. He found it queer looking through a weekly paper with them and 'coming to a picture of the eldest with the label "our future king". Prince Albert at once drew attention to it, but the elder hastily brushed his brother's finger away and turned the page.' It was a curious omen – he turned the page indeed, and it was Albert who reigned as George VI. Unusually observant where boys were concerned, Esher was intrigued by the budding personality of the one who was to become Duke of Windsor. Prince Edward, he notes in 1906, is getting to look more like 'the *old* family every day. He has the mouth and expression of old Queen Charlotte. His memory is remarkable – a family tradition; but the look of *Weltschmerz* in his eyes I cannot trace to any ancestor of the House of Hanover.' Everyone noticed the extraordinary sadness of his eyes in repose; he was certainly not born to be happy – where did this strain come from? One day twenty years later, when the boy had become Prince of Wales, Esher perhaps had a moment of illumination: 'this boy is a Stuart, not a Brunswick'.

In the previous generation there had been a comparable sadness. Edward VII's elder son, Prince Eddy, Duke of Clarence, had the misfortune to fall in love, though respectably, outside the charmed circle of possible marriage: with Hélène, daughter of the Comte de Paris, Pretender to the French throne, who as a Catholic could not marry the heir-presumptive to the English throne, while the Pope would not grant a dispensation to her to turn Protestant. There was already a possible bride at hand in Princess May, a great-granddaughter of George III, whom Queen Victoria approved as a suitable queen-consort one day. So, when Prince Eddy proposed to this rather shy, but remarkable, girl and posted off next day to Windsor for the Queen's sanction, it was readily given and the young couple were taken to the Mausoleum to receive Albert's.

But shortly Prince Eddy died, in January 1893. Upon the elaborate and spreading memorial to him (by Alfred Gilbert), which occupies the place of Wolsey's tomb in the Albert Memorial Chapel, hangs a wreath with the one word 'Hélène'. Princess May's bridal wreath was placed on the coffin at his

George V riding in Windsor Great Park with his sons.

funeral. After the lapse of a suitable interval Eddy's brother, George, in the Duke of Windsor's masculine phrase, 'spoke up for himself', and in due course Princess May took her place in the succession of queen-consorts, as Queen Mary.

Edward VII's short reign, like Victoria's long one, came to an end amid public worries and a political crisis. In his case a constitutional one: he was deeply anxious about the proposal of Asquith's government to create an immense number of peers to flood the Conservative majority in the House of Lords. The King had 'screwed himself up' to invite Asquith to Windsor – who refused! 'He is going abroad. The Queen would never have stood this, but the King is far too good-natured.' The Prime Minister was tired and 'done up'; but it was the King who died.

It fell to Esher to arrange the funeral ceremonies at Windsor, and once more to observe the complete change of atmosphere with a new régime. George V loved to revert to the ways of his grandmother, domestic quiet, simplicity and work. 'We are back in Victorian times. Everything so peaceful and domestic ... The King works in his room all the morning.' None of the social ferment and cosmopolitan bustle surrounding Edward VII. The new king was 'assiduous and conscientious' like Queen Victoria, and liked to concentrate his attention on his work. When Queen Mary said to the children playing in the Corridor that they had better not, 'Father won't like it', the

Prince of Wales at once challenged it: 'I take the responsibility.' Perhaps another portent? – though a more significant one was that of the aviator Sopwith, in February 1911, circling round the Castle and landing on the golf course. Today, the Castle is in view of the thousands of planes arriving at and departing from London Airport, though a wonderful view we all get, equally and democratically, in return.

Queen Mary, with her sense of history and her connoisseurship, adored Windsor Castle. From the moment she entered upon the heritage Lord Esher describes her collecting together its treasures, arranging, cataloguing, spending hours in the Library. She was, indeed, a 'châtelaine of genius'. She had disapproved of Edward VII's precipitate changes and cavalier way with the contents; Queen Victoria had been too lofty to bother, Edward and Alexandra too Philistine to care. The result was that many things had gone astray, been taken by relatives abroad. Queen Mary indefatigably traced them and often got them back; she recovered relegated furniture and *objets d'art* – in her appreciation of the elegance of Regency taste she made a valuable contribution to that of her own time. She was in addition herself a collector; in the Lace Room she brought together a collection of personal belongings and souvenirs of the family, from Queen Charlotte onwards. George VI was able to add to it, since he inherited some of his mother's aptitude and appreciation of needlework and embroideries.

George V and Queen Mary were happy at Windsor; Esher noted his unaffected naturalness and simple dignity: he came upon the King picking primroses on the slopes for Queen Alexandra, 'Mother Dear', or he would pull up on his ride in the Park for a chat – 'the first time I ever knew of a Sovereign doing so simple and homely a thing'. At Windsor George V made an exception from his dislike of entertaining and regularly invited distinguished guests who counted for something in the life of the country and of the Empire – while it yet lasted.

Their last years were clouded by doubts about the future, in particular with regard to the heir to it all. The Duke of Windsor has told us his own story, from his own side, with an edge on it. He describes his creation as Prince of Wales at Windsor on his sixteenth birthday, and next day his confirmation by Archbishop Davidson, who spoke of his 'dedication to the high ideals of Christian manhood'. He was admitted Knight of the Garter in the Garter Room. It was a happy spring, as he remembered, with the trees coming out in the Park.

Quite early he was called in to help in entertaining the visiting royalties. The Kaiser he found essentially humourless; his brother, Prince Henry of Prussia, was friendly to Britain and therefore kept out of the German Higher Command. In November 1913 the Prince of Wales was called to Windsor from Oxford to help to receive the Archduke Franz Ferdinand – whose fate at Sarajevo was not far away. In the spring of 1914 there was the state-visit of the King and

INSTRUMENT OF ABDICATION

I, Edward the Eighth, of Great Britain, Ireland, and the British Dominions beyond the Seas, King, Emperor of India, do hereby declare My irrevocable determination to renounce the Throne for Myself and for My descendants, and My desire that effect should be given to this Instrument of Abdication immediately.

In token whereof I have hereunto set My hand this tenth day of December, nineteen hundred and thirty six, in the presence of the witnesses whose signatures are subscribed.

SIGNED AT
FORT BELVEDERE
IN THE PRESENCE
OF

Edward RI

Albert

Henry

George

The Instrument of Abdication, 'the last scene in the inglorious story took place at Windsor'.

Queen of Denmark. For Ascot week there were always thirty guests, the gold plate out, the band playing, the King and his sons in their Windsor uniforms. In the intervals of these chores the Prince would often look at the Bible General Gordon had on him when speared at Khartoum, a relic Queen Victoria had treasured. But in youth he found the Castle overpowering. Once the young members of the family tried to improvise a dance after the King and Queen had gone to bed; it was a failure – the very walls disapproved.

He came to appreciate the Castle more when he made Fort Belvedere his own, the place most associated with his 'romance' that made history, though there was nothing particularly romantic about it. The last word on the subject was written by his mother, Queen Mary: 'you did not seem able to take in any point of view but your own ... I do not think you have ever realised the shock, which the attitude you took up caused your family and the whole Nation. It seemed inconceivable to those who had made such sacrifices during the war that you, as their King, refused a lesser sacrifice.' There is a finality from which there is no appeal in that sentence. His brother 'dreaded' taking on the burden of kingship: he was a charming man of good courage, with simple tastes, a sense of humour and native wit. He made a far better king as George vi.

The last scenes in the unglamorous story took place at Windsor. Having made his decision to abdicate, driving back to Fort Belvedere, Edward viii caught a glimpse of the great Castle standing solid and changeless, making its own comment on his affair. It stood for the continuity of history, for secular duty, from which abdication was a dereliction. After handing over, he made his farewell broadcast to the nation he was leaving, from the Castle. 'The great quadrangle was dark and deserted as we entered. Only at the Sovereign's Entrance was there light and activity. A few of the officials of the Castle, among them my father's old Private Secretary, Lord Wigram – in his dual capacity of Deputy Constable and Lieutenant-Governor of the Castle – received me at the doors. I mounted the Gothic staircase to my old rooms in the Augusta Tower ...'

The broadcast we all heard was delivered. Many wept that night. The Prince returned to take leave of his brothers; as George vi recorded, 'when David and I said goodbye we kissed, parted as freemasons, and he bowed to me as his King'. Duty was resumed.

The Duke, who chose to pass the rest of his life in exile, ardently desired at the last that his body be brought home to Windsor.

There the symbol remains, up on the horizon, a great grey cliff of many memories, standing above the swirling waters of our time, a civilisation undermined and breaking up, in transformation we do not know to what.

Index

Index